FUSE

FUSE

MAKING SENSE *of the* NEW COGENERATIONAL WORKPLACE™

JIM FINKELSTEIN

with MARY GAVIN

GREENLEAF
BOOK GROUP PRESS

Published by Greenleaf Book Group Press
Austin, Texas
www.gbgpress.com

First published in 2009 by Booksurge as *Fuse: Igniting the Full Power of the Creative Economy*

www.fusethebook.com

Distributed by Greenleaf Book Group LLC

For ordering information or special discounts for bulk purchases, please contact Greenleaf Book Group LLC at PO Box 91869, Austin, TX 78709, 512.891.6100.

Design and composition by Greenleaf Book Group LLC
Cover design by Greenleaf Book Group LLC

Publisher's Cataloging-In-Publication Data
(Prepared by The Donohue Group, Inc.)
Finkelstein, Jim.
Fuse : making sense of the new cogenerational workplace / Jim Finkelstein with Mary Gavin. — 1st ed.
p. ; cm.
Includes bibliographical references and index.
ISBN: 978-1-60832-146-9
1. Diversity in the workplace—United States. 2. Age groups—United States. 3. Intergenerational relations—United States. 4. Personnel management. I. Gavin, Mary (Mary K.), 1954- II. Title.
HF5549.5.M5 F56 2011
658.3/008 2011931381

Part of the Tree Neutral® program, which offsets the number of trees consumed in the production and printing of this book by taking proactive steps, such as planting trees in direct proportion to the number of trees used: www.treeneutral.com

TreeNeutral®

Printed in the United States of America on acid-free paper

11 12 13 14 15 16 10 9 8 7 6 5 4 3 2 1

Second Edition

ACKNOWLEDGMENTS

This book is dedicated to all those cogenerational workers who have already found the creative genius in each other and a way to use it in the workplace—from the Seniors who are texting up a storm, to the Boomers who are trying to reenter the workforce after one of the most devastating recessions in our history, to the recently graduated Millennials who are entering the workforce for the first time—all of whom still need to make a basic living. We look to them, the Senioroomergenxennials, to inspire us all.

Our first vote of thanks goes to our *Fuse* team—a cogenerational group themselves—who with perspicacity, persistence, and patience, collaborated to create a better manuscript. They were researchers, thinkers, and constructive commentators.

The FUSE Team

The Boomers: Ayelet Baron, Alana Capozzi, and Amy Damianakes.

The Millennials: Matt Finkelstein, Kyle Jaimerena, Zoe Jarocki, Melissa K. Mead, and Heather Stout.

We also thank our FutureSense colleagues, Margaret Walker, Kyle Jaimerena, Sheila McDaniel and Regan Poston for their insights and support.

And we thank and honor the heart and soul of an author's cheering section—our families, two- and four-legged. Lynn, Matt, Brett, Kahala, and Ernie; Tim, Steve, and Sarei—thank you for your constant love and belief in our ideas.

Finally, we honor those who are dedicated to transforming the twentieth-century workplace into an environment much more relevant to the twenty-first-century workforce; those who recognize that we have moved beyond the Industrial and Information ages to one of the most creative renaissances in our history; those who are willing to look beyond the traditional and known to the untried and unknown; and ultimately those who will take the time to find an *aha!* or two in our book and apply it in their working lives.

—Jim Finkelstein and Mary Gavin

CONTENTS

TERMS OF ENDEARMENT

NAMES FOR THE NEWEST GENERATION OF WORKERS

ADHD Generation
Adultolescents
Boomer Babies
Boomerang Generation
Cynical Generation
D.A.R.E. Generation
Digital Natives
DIY Generation
Echo Boomers
Gamers
Generation 2.0
Generation 2000
Generation 9/11
Generation C *(Connected)*
Generation.com
Generation Next
Generation Me
Generation Tech
Generation Whiner
Generation Why
Generation Y
Generation XX
Google Generation
iGeneration
KIPPERS *(Kids in Parents' Pockets Eroding Retirement Savings)*
Millennials
MyPod Generation
MySpace Generation
Net Generation
Next (or Second) Greatest Generation
Nintendo Generation
Peter Pan Generation
Reagan Babies
Second Baby Boom
Trophy Generation
YGen

NAMES FOR THE SOON-TO-BE RETIRING* GENERATION

Baby Boomers

Generation Jones

Hippies

Largest and Richest Generation

Love Generation

Me Generation

Now Generation

Pig in the Python Generation

Sandwich Generation

Shockwave Generation

Self-Absorbed Generation

Spock Generation

TV Generation

*Maybe

FOREWORD

By John Caple, Ph.D.

"Know thyself," the sages advise. And they also like its corollary, "Know thy neighbor." Excellent advice, especially if you're a CEO or marketing executive and your neighbor is a prospective customer for your goods and services, or a prospective employee. The more you know, the more effective you become.

In *Fuse,* Jim Finkelstein, Mary Gavin, and their collaborators write from this perennial wisdom. They provide two key perspectives: first, to help you as an employee become more aware of others around you (no matter your generation), and second, to help you as an employer or leader learn how to "mash up" the best of all cogenerational workers and create the best workplaces.

In *Fuse,* employees will learn how to create, connect, and survive, and employers will learn new ways to identify the most productive people they employ. This is not another "generations" book that just talks about all the differences; rather, it seeks to find the *fusions*—the common components that exist in all of us, whether Millennial or Boomer. And Jim Finkelstein has lived this in his own life—as an employee, a parent, a coach, and an employer of Millennials for the past fifteen years. He is a self-avowed Millennial in Boomer clothing.

Fuse is really a blog between covers. It is the SparkNotes (Millennials) or CliffsNotes (Boomers) version of the mash-up between the twentieth-century workplace and the twenty-first-century workforce. It presents information in accessible, byte-size chunks for those with short attention spans. It is opinionated and often irreverent and offers a lot of the best current thinking on generational interaction.

Fuse is as timeless and enduring as *Passages* by Gail Sheehy. It is as informative about adult development (yes, Millennials in the workplace are adults) as *The Seasons of a Man's Life* by Daniel J. Levinson. It is an outstanding book. As you turn the pages that follow, prepare to be enlightened, engaged, amused, and motivated to leverage change in your own workplace.

—John Caple,
author of *Finding the Hat That Fits*

Forward!

"The last few decades have belonged to a certain kind of person with a certain kind of mind—computer programmers who could crank code, lawyers who could craft contracts, MBAs who could crunch numbers. But the keys to the kingdom are changing hands. The future belongs to a very different kind of person with a very different kind of mind—creators and empathizers, pattern recognizers, and meaning makers. These people . . . will now reap society's richest rewards."

—Daniel Pink

The playwright Anton Chekhov once wrote, "If you cry 'Forward' you must be sure to make clear the direction in which to go. . . . If you fail to do that and simply call out the word to a monk and a revolutionary, they will go in precisely opposite directions." Substitute "Boomer" and "Millennial" for the words "monk" and "revolutionary." You'll get a pretty accurate picture of how these two characters are being scripted in the reality show of our current workforce. Polarized, radically different—and certainly not able to play in the sandbox of business together!

Generational books are flying off bookstore shelves and e-book servers. Most proclaim that the Boomers are retiring, the Millennials are inheriting the business world, and a calamity will befall us through this attrition and accession. Boomers are obsolete, with one foot in the grave, and Millennials are the entitled, self-centered generation. Tamara Erickson summed up the consensus on Millennials in her book *Retire Retirement:*[1] "They seem, to many Boomers, to have ridiculous expectations of the level of responsibility that they'll be given and little willingness to pay their dues . . . fearless and blunt, they offer their opinions freely, without regard for corporate hierarchy and with no sense of what would be considered 'proper' business protocol—and they expect everyone to be interested in their point of view."

We use Millennials and Boomers as our bookends because their sheer numbers dominate the workplace and because they fill the roles of peons and bosses at this point in time. And economic woes that slashed 401(k)s to 201(k)s mean that they will spend more time working together as Boomers are forced to delay retirement. Clearly, as Boomers assess both their Dr. Oz–inspired longevity and their lack of assets to support their longer life span, many, like the Energizer Bunny, will keep going . . . and going . . . and going . . . for much longer than they think.

It is a brave new world. When Daniel Pink proclaimed the end of the Information Age in his book *A Whole New Mind*[2] most of us in the Boomer generation shrugged, slightly embarrassed that we hadn't caught that wave the first time.

Yes, we knew that technology was changing the world. We ourselves used the Internet for emails, real-time sports news, and comparison shopping. Yes, our kids at school and at work had their noses not to the grindstone but to LCD displays. And yes, the young people our companies were hiring seemed bizarrely competent and confident, given their lack of maturity and experience. But Boomers have long defined the world—including the realms of work, politics, relationships, consumerism, religion, and art—in our own terms, by our own reflections.

If we didn't invent it, grow it, think it, or perceive it, it didn't exist.

Enter the Millennials—the iGeneration, Generation Y, the Gamers, the Digital Natives, whatever you want to call all 80 million Americans born between 1980 and 1995. They process information differently than the rest of us—conceptually, in parallel processes, looking not particularly for answers but for options. Their generation has unique skills. Weaned on video games and touchscreens, they are competitive, competent, collaborative, passionate, persistent, and self-possessed. Their unique mind-set is based largely on almost *universal experience with technology*, an experience not shared by any other generation.

The Millennial generation is changing the world of work. Consequently, our premise is this: *Organizations need to create a mash-up of the twentieth-century workplace and the twenty-first-century workforce.*

A mash-up is information and presentation separated and remixed to create novel forms of reuse. It's an organic form of innovation that's evolved because the democratization and speed of information of the World Wide Web has dissolved boundaries between disciplines.

The *Fuse* mash-up is a combination of the experience, command, and linearity of Boomers and the techno-smart, collaborative, and boundary-less thought of Millennials. The result will be people connecting and creating in a new, collaborative, community-driven, Cogenerational Workplace™. The Millennial/Boomer mash-up—a *fusion* of their unique perspectives and abilities—will increase innovation, service levels, and productivity, and will dramatically reduce time to market.

We believe that the wisdom and experience of the Boomers, combined with the savvy and boundless energy of the Millennials, will help inspire a new workforce culture, one in which conversations about generational differences are replaced by an understanding of how the blend of talents makes for a more effective and efficient frontier—a new kind of corporate sweet talk. It is all about having the right conversation, one that doesn't polarize but instead engages and embraces the assets. When you do that, *voilà*! You create the possibilities for a new level of productivity and success.

In *Fuse*, we detail how Millennials are demonstrably different from other generations in their thinking, expectations, resourcefulness, and results. They are more psychological and emotional and less pragmatic than other generations at work. They do not perceive boundaries of time, space, age, gender, race, ownership, or country of origin. They create their own learning experiences by being an integral part of the content they interact with. They favor random access over hierarchy and linearity. And they effortlessly use technology to bring bodies of knowledge, modes of thought, and abstract ideas to life.

We believe that their culture is the petri dish of true innovation.

In *Fuse*, we also honor how Boomers created the workplace as it exists today. We try to make clear the enormous strength Boomers bring to the following equation:

Twentieth-century workplace +
twenty-first-century workforce =
a more robust, creative, and compelling economy

Boomers provide knowledge, resources, stability, and implementation skills. They model behaviors for Millennials, from customer service to corporate responsibility. They are passionate about the social causes they embrace, as well as their generation's conviction that each person can make a difference.

And they have proven that they can change the world:

American Boomers ended the Vietnam War, pioneered racial parity, swept women into universities and workplaces, and explored outer space.

Boomers and Millennials must first understand themselves and then understand each other. Mutual understanding is crucial: the relationship between the generations is the fuse that will ignite the full power of our economy.

To inspire and motivate people to truly understand each other works better than relying on generalizations about generations. In this book, we've tried to embody the spirit of "seek to understand rather than to be understood." There are no statements or judgments that one generation is better or smarter than the other. Rather, we seek to honor the unique gifts and contributions of both.

That each generation has unique value seems obvious. So why does it require yet another guidebook, another primer for the twenty-first century?

- Because the needs of Millennials are different from Boomers' in terms of work styles, risk-taking, rewards, and ROI. This translates to the Millennials' collective inability to find a clear, satisfying career path (if they can even get a job); to the 80 percent rate of job dissatisfaction; to the high cost of turnover ($75,000 per turn); and to the Boomers' inability to reenter the workforce.
- Because organizations—managed largely by Boomers—will have to tolerate and leverage

Millennial workers in upcoming years; 64 million skilled Boomers are still trying to retire by the end of the decade.

- Because the workplace itself—the environment and context of getting the job done—is being transformed by information technology, 2.0 tools, multilevel data streams, 24/7 business hours, brutal global competition, and plain old speed.
- Because today's workplace change is exponential, not the incremental change of the past. It is fast, it is furious, and it can be fatal to organizations and people that cannot understand how to leverage it to their advantage.

This book has been informed by many sources:

- More than a hundred years of collective experience on the part of the authors and our collaborators
- Case studies of client problems
- A nationwide survey detailing Millennials' workplace attitudes and aspirations
- Substantive research into current workplace mores and modalities
- A great deal of thoughtful concern and discourse with educators and change leaders about the students and workers of the present and the workplace of the future

- Good old-fashioned common sense, tempered by a bit of nostalgia for the hierarchical, Boomer-built workplaces fast receding into the past
- A great deal of eager anticipation for the organic, evolutionary, mashed-up workplaces of the present and the future

Our intention was to keep this book simple and relatively short. We wanted to cover topics that are important to both generations. We write to be helpful to employees and employers, to individual contributors such as the new cadre of "just-in-time" contractors, and to thought leaders. Our chapters are shout-outs of much more extended and deep conversations regarding some of the most crucial components of being successful (as either employee or employer) in this mashed-up, cogenerational workforce. We include the voices of Boomers and Millennials, with special contributions by Melissa K. Mead representing the Millennial perspective, and Boomer Ayelet Baron, who leads strategy for Cisco Systems Canada, filling in the blanks of social media usage for novices and experts alike.

We've put "Fuse Factoids" throughout the book to call out culled data that provides some of the footings for our work. We also present "Fuse Tips" in every chapter to help employers look at their people—Boomers and Millennials—differently. Presented as sound bites, they can be used as discussion topics throughout organizations, and for on-the-spot changes in workplace routines. In addition, at the end of each chapter we set out the "Fusions" from that chapter—the places where there are more generational similarities than differences, where there are opportunities to recognize that the workforce of the future will be even more cogenerational than ever before (you could literally be working with both your grandparents' best friends *and* your kids' BFFs at the same time). These Fusions also reveal the challenges that require leveraging the unique gifts (and mitigating the annoying attributes) of each generation.

We intended to write a book that is analytical yet at the same time conveys practical suggestions. "You" is truly the reader—Seniors, Boomers, Gen-Xers, Millennials; employees and employers; interested students of human behavior, and people simply on a journey to discover new ideas and to expand old ones. We have been told by Boomers and Millennials alike that one of the most interesting revelations after reading *Fuse* is that it expanded their consciousness, not just about the other generation, but also significantly about *themselves*.

Every point in this book will not apply to every Millennial, or to every Boomer. There is a great deal of personal individuation within the generations—regional and cultural differences, gender anomalies, etc. Yet there are such strong trend lines within the groups that our topics are useful both in the general and in the particular. We chose the chapter subjects by virtue of the challenges they present in the workplace today. Each topic is key to creating the workplace of tomorrow.

The chapters culminate in the topic of innovation and the future, and in our deeply held belief that we haven't seen anything yet. Whatever your service or product line, the innovations that will be brought by a wholly leveraged, cogenerational workforce will fuel twenty-first-century creativity, productivity, and profitability.

We encourage you to browse the notes section in the back of the book for a deeper investigation into the topics we cover. We strongly recommend in particular the seminal works on generations in the workplace by William Strauss and Neil Howe, on gamers by John C. Beck and Mitchell Wade, on mobilizing Generation 2.0 by Ben Rigby, and on Generation Me by Jean M. Twenge. We also recommend anything written by Marc Prensky, McCrindle Research, or Penelope Trunk and Ryan Healy in their Brazen Careerist clothing.[3]

Fuse is not static. Please send us survey responses, comments, and ideas for Fusions and Fuse Tips at www.fusethebook.com. Most of all we'd like you to answer the question: *What is the one new thing that you are thinking about because you read this book?* You can also write a blog post or comment on another post to keep the dialogue going. Many thanks.

CHAPTER 1

Slackers, Superheroes, or Superfluous?

"You can't connect the dots looking forward; you can only connect them looking backwards. So you have to trust that the dots will somehow connect in your future."
—Steve Jobs

So, what are these bookend working generations all about? Are they egocentric, egotistical, essential, exasperating, or all of the above? Are they

- Slackers—either wanting everything now or coasting until they retire?
- Superheroes—either inventors and innovators or inspirers?

- Superfluous—either stuck in the cradle or obsolete, with one foot in the grave?

Let's start with Millennials. There is little debate about the attributes of Millennial workers, but there is furious disagreement over how to decode those attributes in the workplace.

Millennials are the 80 million or so Americans roughly between the ages of fifteen and thirty[1]—those born between 1980 and 1995. More than 50 million are old enough to start a career. They have grown up wired. Electronic media is their primary source of learning, producing, and—often—interacting. Many prefer texting to talking.

Each generation is different from the ones before it, because environment shapes individual and group behavior, but this generation is manifestly different because it has been shaped not by understanding the natural world and manipulating its resources but by artificial intelligence and virtual relationships. Marc Prensky writes in *strategy+business* magazine: "They communicate . . . meet . . . play games, learn, evolve, search, analyze . . . socialize, explore, and even transgress using new digital methods and a new vocabulary most older managers don't even understand. Blog? Wiki? RTS? Spawn? POS? Astroturf? How do these sound when juxtaposed with cross-functional cooperation, team-based management, and 360 feedback?"[2] There are more Millennials than Boomers, and their sheer numbers and unique norms are changing the social and business landscape. As is true of land armies, the larger the force, the more likely the victory. Millennials will outlast and, of course, outlive Boomers.

But they can't declare victory just yet. Many Millennials are having a tough time finding employment and are not yet replacing Boomers. They are moving back in with their parents in droves—even as married couples. According to a Pew Research Center survey, "Thirteen percent of parents with grown children recently reported that an adult son or daughter had moved home in the past year. Of those, 2 in 10 were full-time students and one-quarter were unemployed. About one-third had lived on their own before returning home." Reoccupying the empty nest is becoming another stop along the flight path to true independence.

With no source of income, a lot of Millennials are going back to or staying in school. Many are earning master's degrees and finding that their new credentials are not of great help in their field of choice. In fact, an advanced degree may actually be hindering them in getting interim jobs. So in their free time, they are volunteering, taking internships, and otherwise trying to gain transferable experience. And, they are also amassing large amounts of debt. So Boomers can relax for a while!

Yet, despite this hiccup in the marketplace, how are Millennials so different from their predecessors, especially as employees?

Millennials are individuals, of course, with unique character traits and novel sensibilities; they're not a homogeneous demographic. Every distribution curve has a tail, and in the United States, people on the coasts differ from those in the central and southern states—in dress, in expectations on the job, in exposure to nonhierarchical institutions, and in many other ways. However, Millennials are almost universally perceived as tech-savvy, project-oriented multitaskers and as competitive gamers who enjoy risk and court reward passionately. They are collaborative, color-blind, and socially conscious. Their choices focus on output, not method. They learn experientially, by trial and error. Philosophically speaking, to borrow a phrase from *Megatrends* author John Naisbitt, "They balance the material wonders of technology with the spiritual demands of our human nature."[3]

Another broad-brush view paints a picture of Millennials as self-centered, shortsighted, high-maintenance, and ignorant of cultural and social mores. They want instant gratification, from feedback to promotions. That ravenous appetite is fed by the instant responses of text messaging, which some research tells us create the same dopamine release as recreational drugs. Their focus is on balancing their life to achieve the greatest happiness. They question everything from a position of undifferentiated equality and have supremely unrealistic expectations. They are loud, pierced, entitled, and unapologetic.

FUSE TIP

Highly educated Millennials may come across as egotistical know-it-alls. But it's okay to hire smart alecks. Look past the noise so you don't miss out on what may be some of the most innovative and productive employees you'll ever hire.

Their Boomer managers, who have shaped the workplace and the workforce in their own image, just don't understand what makes this generation tick. The lack of understanding portends a very poor outcome for both groups.

Because the average worker replacement cost is $75,000, not understanding the new generation of workers is an extremely expensive exercise in futility.[4] So let's do a little decoding of this new generation.

The pros and cons of the Millennial generation are laid out in the books *Got Game*, by John C. Beck and Mitchell Wade, and *Generation Me*, by Jean M. Twenge.[5] Both detail the Millennial mentality, but they come to wildly disparate conclusions.

Got Game claims that gamers will rewrite global business, based on the unique gaming skills of risk-taking, reward-seeking, and goal-scoring and the ability to infinitely replay or reset situations until victory is achieved.

Generation Me, on the other hand, looks to fill in the territory between soaring expectations and crushing realities, detailing the Millennials' bouts of uncertainty, anxiety, and depression despite the highest levels of support, education, and opportunity in history.

Both sets of conclusions are drawn from solid data: *Got Game* is based on two thousand detailed survey responses taken by Millennials in a five-year span, and *Generation Me* is based on psychological survey data from 1.3 million young Americans over four decades.

In fact, Millennials are neither saints nor sinners, slackers nor superfluous.

They are a cohort of employees with unique skills and a mind-set that enables them—if led well and managed to potential—to change for the better the way business is done around the world.

FUSE TIP

Change is painful. Don't expect everyone in your organization to immediately embrace Millennial attitudes. Help the naysayers appreciate the value of acceptance, and make sure you value it too. As Beck and Wade say in *Got Game,* "Reality changed much faster than our attitudes." Make sure that yours are up-to-date.

The first thing to do is to *understand them*. Boomers may never fathom Millennials completely, but it's important that they share part of their younger counterparts' perspective. Boomers love to tell tales of Millennials' narcissism and sense of entitlement, because it makes Boomers look so good by comparison. But *Millennial attributes are neither right nor wrong*, even when measured against Boomer expectations. They are just different.

Consider the effect of video games on this generation. Beck and Wade say, "What gives digital games the power to transform practical life is that they have been adopted wholesale by people of one age group and largely ignored by everyone older than that." Video games offer an alternative reality that has given Millennials (and Gen-Xers) ways of working, skills, and goals in life that are not shared by older workers. Gaming is a $60–$70 billion industry worldwide, with thousands of titles produced a year. Ninety-two percent of Millennials play them. Gamer values have infiltrated Millennial culture and are now being brought into the workplace.[6]

To the Boomers reading this book we pose this question: Have you *ever* played a video game? Take a small personal risk and just do it. It doesn't matter if you play with a Wii or an Xbox 360 or PlayStation 3 or smartphone. You can ask about game systems and games at major big box outlets, or you can go to an electronics store and leverage the experience of the staff. They'll fix you up with the virtual reality equivalent of a blind date—just you and a few strange video games. It will undoubtedly be an eye-opening experience.

In addition to a gamer mentality, *entitlement* is another Millennial trait that drives Boomer managers crazy.

Is it real? Yes.

Is it a valid point of contention? No.

Most Millennials are products of the self-esteem movement. They were weaned on limitless parental praise and attended schools whose goals were to instill individual expression and personal happiness. Every morning, Barney the big purple dinosaur told them they were special. All participants on athletic teams got medals. Everyone who did the work got an A. Trying was as good as achieving. Millennial workers are the result of this culture, and they can demand a lot of attention.

FUSE FACTOIDS

- Younger employees report 600 percent more job dissatisfaction than older employees do; 80 percent of Millennials dislike their jobs.
- The average Millennial will have 8.6 jobs between the ages of eighteen and thirty-two.

For Boomer managers seeking to acculturate Millennial workers, it's best to gently disabuse them of the notion that they are the center of the universe. Keep in mind that even Aristotle got the planetary alignment wrong. The effort will pay off. As one employer remarked: "This is the most high-maintenance workforce in the world. The good news is that they're also going to be the most high-performing."[7]

If your patience is wearing thin, remind yourself of the average turnover cost per Millennial employee: $75,000.

Then go one step further in your effort to make the most of Millennial colleagues and turn their eagerness for praise to your advantage. If you see that they are motivated by positive feedback, give it to them. Words are cheap. Just make sure your comments are authentic, so that they are not perceived to be phony or manipulative. And be aware of the flip side of praise: Criticism is not likely to be taken well. Or taken at all. That's the downside of bulletproof self-esteem.

FUSE TIP

Revamp your employee reward and recognition programs. Skip the gold watches. Rewards that please Millennials will probably cost less but mean more. Time off, flextime, pro bono work, networking opportunities, and concert tickets are all great motivators.

Of course, being oblivious of or impervious to criticism is not unique to Millennials. While working as the assistant to the CEO of the biggest bank in the country, one of the authors of this book thought that instruction offered by the boss in casual conversation was optional, or at least open to discussion. Only after the CEO pointed out that the workplace was not a democracy did it sink in: The workplace is not a democracy. Listening to what senior coworkers say is crucial. Make it clear to your Millennial workers that they need to pay attention, as even casual conversation contains feedback, cues, and clues to workplace success.

When negative feedback for Millennials is necessary, Boomers should start with praise and offer the context for criticism. Start with the good news, then the constructive commentary, such as, "That was a good first effort, but did you consider the possibility of including x and y?" Often, framing the constructive commentary as questions, not as judgmental statements, will make a difference in feedback as a motivator, particularly for Millennials who may have been only softly criticized in their learning experience. Frame the criticism in a positive and constructive manner—e.g., "this is in the best interest of the company" or "this will really help the progress of your own career." Then be specific, pinpoint the situation, and explain the consequence of the behavior that needs to change. Explaining the problem's impact on the employee, the manager, the department, and the company helps transform criticism into useful feedback.

If the defensive card is played, don't trump it. It may

take a while to have normal managerial conversations; many Millennials are strangers to criticism. But most love feedback, the quicker the better.

How I Learned Things in Kindergarten

Boomers methodically learned the facts they would need to pass the test. Millennials learned through constant connection, multitasking, co-creation, and shared experiences. They use experiential trial and error, constantly checking their network feedback and actively creating the learning experience.

FUSE TIP

Embrace some failure. It is a sure sign that Millennials are learning.

The best way to bring these ends together is for both generations to be proactive. Coach each other! Jack Welch was famous for insisting on this at General Electric company. Cisco, a company that describes itself as "the worldwide leader in networking that transforms how people connect, communicate, and collaborate," has a robust reverse-mentoring program. This is detailed in our bonus chapter by

Cisco strategist Ayelet Baron. In your workplace, even if the mentoring is heavily weighted in one direction, there will be a feedback loop that leverages individual strengths—which will increase as the time colleagues spend mentoring increases.

In "Learning Along with Millennials," Russ Eckel notes a particularly successful example of how cogenerational working adds to the bottom line: "Deloitte & Touche has implemented a training and career development and career management system that recognizes the primacy of learning as a core value of young workers. Managing the generational mix has resulted in hundreds of young workers staying at Deloitte, with a declared savings of one hundred million dollars."[8]

The way Millennials learn can directly benefit organizations in another way. Rapid change, relentless global competition, and exploding complexity have turned even mundane decisions into problems of true uncertainty. Boomers need to understand that Millennials already live in a complex data space that they can manipulate at will, and that they are comfortable handling a multitude of simultaneous data streams. As Beck and Wade note in *Got Game,* "A professional workforce used to two-dimensional thinking now faces an *n*-dimensional world."

Cutting-edge analytic tools that explore real-world "what if" scenarios—in finance, engineering, risk analysis, climate change, etc.—operate the same way video games do. Using them is a purely digital, interactive experience.

There is no bottom line, no final report. They create value by helping teams explore operational uncertainties. Maybe limiting playing time for our gamers was a bad idea. Who would have guessed they were honing valuable analytical skills and the ability to think and respond quickly?

These analytical tools are the future in real time, and their benefits are best delivered by the only generation that truly understands how to use them.

What Millennials don't understand is the workplace—its constructs, constraints, and culture. All their lives they've had coaches for every physical skill and mentors for every intellectual interest. In the workplace, they need guides to help them learn corporate culture, guides who will bridge the generation gap, guides who will show them how to interpret communication.

Boomers can step right into those starring roles.

How? It's useful to start by getting some solid information about the demographics of your organization. Do a quick age profile to make sure you understand who's working for you. If you understand their various motivational profiles, you can implement ways to develop their skills, harness their energy, and promote mutual coaching. This will go a long way toward employee actualization and will help you avoid or minimize the substantial costs of conflicts and turnover—to say nothing of developing bench strength to cover your eventual Boomer retirements. (Although there's no rocking chair in sight for the majority of Boomers just yet.)

As Boomers negotiate a working relationship with the upcoming generations, they would be wise to heed this advice: "Don't waste time wishing your Millennial employees were different. . . . These employees are not a reflection of you, nor are they an earlier version of you. . . . Your task is to take this new understanding and use it to reposition how you interact with, motivate, and reward your staff." [9]

Millennials Slackers? I Don't Think So!

A contribution from

MILLENNIAL MELISSA K. MEAD

The word "automobile" is too long. Therefore, every day we get into our *cars*. We get in the fast lane. We drive to work. We strive for the middle ground between quality and quantity, as well as speed and accuracy. We *jet* everywhere. In case anyone was wondering, no longer does the word "jet" only refer to a blisteringly loud, turbo-fast aircraft. In *our* minds (the minds of Millennials, that is) to "jet" implies rapid movement from destination to destination.

Some may find this strange, but we hardly *ever* imagine wasting a second of our day. Of course, the definition of "wasting time" will forever be disputable. Some of our most "successful" days would be (naturally) deemed such by how much we squeezed into them, as well as the quality of all that content. Between the vibrations of our iPhones playfully tweeting away and the echo of our Bluetooth headsets, there's never a dull moment en route to our daily terminuses. Nor do we desire one. Go figure. We are a generation that is entirely comfortable with taking both risks and shortcuts to achieve success. The more intuitive, the better!

But the person who will (more often than not) opt for taking the long way, merely because it's the correct, foolproof, and trustworthy way, is the very person whom my generation fails to completely understand. More important, these are the people my generation fails to *attempt* to understand. They are, of course, the Boomers.

Millennials "learn by always being connected, by multitasking, [and] by sharing experiences using a wide range of communications technology."[10] And because so many Boomers use the tools we do on only a limited basis or not at all, it's no surprise that we find ourselves questioning whether understanding Boomers is even possible. For Millennials, it's more than easy to not understand them.

We're two incredibly distinct groups of people; it's only natural that we have difficulty understanding one another. Our minds operate in completely different fashions. I'm certainly not the first to admit that Millennials and Boomers argue and disagree all the time when it comes to developing game plans, setting goals, or agreeing how to look at life in general.

The Boomers may be right about some things, but I doubt they really and truly had to walk forty blocks to school—barefoot, in the snow, without a jacket. However, whether we like to admit it or not, there's no denying that the Boomer generation came before that of the Millennials and has many hard-won lessons to teach undeveloped employees. In fact, realistically, Millennials wouldn't be *anywhere* without the foundations the Boomer generation established in the workplace.

As Sally Kane notes in her article "Baby Boomers," for the most part, Boomers are known to be "well-established in their careers and hold positions of power and authority," resulting from "sacrific[ing] a great deal to get where they are in their careers." [11]

Boomers are a generation of work-centric, independent, goal-oriented, and competitive beings. And as far as they're concerned, new challenges are entirely welcome. This competitive nature of theirs stems from linking hierarchy with self-worth. How do I say this quick and painlessly? Okay: the fact that Boomers are so indebted to hierarchical structure and authority often frustrates us Millennials.

But why? We're not frustrated with Boomers themselves. We're mostly frustrated with how they perceive *us*! Yes!

It only makes sense that Boomers (aka the workaholic generation) wholeheartedly believe that youthful Millennials lack work ethic and commitment—do I hear the hiss of the *s* in slacker?—and that they should jump on the societal busy-bee bandwagon, because they themselves grew up thriving on the motivations of position, perks, and prestige. They grew up without the technology that we (basically) rely on. I can't imagine a day without the Internet. In fact, just the other day, my younger sister was complaining about looking up a few facts online for a research project. Consequently, I couldn't *help* but bring up the fact that there was a time when (believe it or not) the Internet didn't exist and that she may well have been flipping through the pages of an encyclopedia at the library if it hadn't been invented.

The Boomers in today's workplace must admit they've learned a thing or two from their younger colleagues. Thanks to a handful of rambunctious Millennials, modes of communication (including Facebook and LinkedIn) have allowed the masses to connect with one another through that lovely portal we like to call the Internet. What would we do without it nowadays?

One thing Boomers really have a handle on (and a big reason why they're still superheroes in *my* book) is the art of what I like to call "meaningful connections." Boomers understand the continuing importance and vitality of face time, otherwise known as your basic, um, human interaction.

While email has become the more popular way of connecting with coworkers, it has also become known as the easy way out, if you catch my drift. I often find myself drafting an email instead of tackling a tough conversation face-to-face. I'm not sure whether it's the nurturing pulse of the cursor on the blank page or the fact that no other soul will hear or even *know* of what I have to say until I click Send.

But honestly, even though it seems professional, it's the easy way out. Any Boomer would agree with me. In fact, any Millennial would too.

While we don't always like to admit it, the best and most efficient mode of communication is talking, not to mention listening (still one of the hardest skills in today's known universe). Try it sometime. Shut up. It's truly liberating.

The qualities of Boomers don't necessarily label them with an expiration sticker, like the ones we use to label foods at Starbucks, where I work. Baby Boomers *aren't* perishable foods. They don't have one foot in the grave (as some people think). Even in the eyes of Millennials, Boomers aren't on their way out the door. Yes, Boomers may use outdated terminology and jargon, but the majority of their intentions and goals are entirely modern, and the majority of what Boomers tell Millennials is based solely on first-hand work experience, as well as pure dedication and years of commitment to their professional accomplishments.

What we need to understand, regardless of whether we're dealing with Boomers or Millennials, is that even the most stubborn of people are still human. Even though we've grown up in different time periods, we Millennials can be just as obstinate as any Boomer. But when we join forces, our collaborative ideas and efforts are incredibly effective. Relatively speaking, at least in terms of age and generation, adults in society's workplace today aren't as incompatible as we perceive them to be.

Millennials and Boomers have more in common than they suspect. They share activist values, goal orientation, and worldview. They can actively help each other with generation-specific advice and practical skills–office politics and management from the Boomers, and technology and transparency from the Millennials. Meeting and mentoring have to start with respect and curiosity. Organizations that can fuse their cogenerational values and skills will lead innovation, customer focus, and productivity. Otherwise, as John Maxwell wisely put it, "If you're leading, and no one's following, then you're just out for a walk."

CHAPTER 1 **FUSIONS**

- Millennial attributes are neither right nor wrong, even when measured against Boomer expectations. They are just different.
- Understanding the difference in learning styles—Boomers learned the facts to pass the test, Millennials create their learning experiences—will reduce turnover and increase organizational resources.

- Do a quick age scan of your workforce to understand who's working for you and their various motivational profiles.
- Have Boomers and Millennials coach each other, even if it's only a 90/10 or even an 80/20 overlap of understanding. They will leverage each other's strengths.

CHAPTER 2

Getting You and Keeping You

"Unique to this generation, technological advances of their lifetimes have given them a jackpot of choices. . . . This means that they will question workplace policies and culture from dress codes to work schedules, and know that there are other options if they are not satisfied with the answers."[1]

Can an organization be both Millennial and Boomer friendly at the same time? Absolutely. Even in a tight job market, it's wise for employees to find a place that fits who they are and what's important to them. As a McCrindle Research report put it: "[Millennials] don't seek a job as much as they seek an opportunity. They have multiple expectations of an organization—it isn't just the job description but the workplace culture, the variety, fun, training, management style, and flexibility that drives them."[2]

Imagine a super-productive Millennial worker who will bring twenty-first-century innovation and profitability to the company lucky enough to hire him. How does the company get so lucky? By using recruiters with piercings or tattoos? No, the employer simply needs to understand, accept, and mirror the Millennial's key needs in its recruitment strategies. They have to be the honey that makes Millennials swarm to their organization. And, they need to look for employees in the places employees will be looking for jobs. As one expert put it: "If you are able to create an environment that embraces the strengths of Millennials, then you will become an employer of clear choice. You can't be chosen unless you're a choice."[3]

Recruiting Millennials and Boomers

Here are some ways Millennial-friendly companies attract and retain talent. As you read through them, you'll also get a perspective on how Boomers view the same issues.

It All Starts with the First Sentence of the Job Description

A Millennial won't read past the first sentence of a job description unless it hooks her. If the first line doesn't explain why the organization is great and how it is making a difference in the community, city, county, state, country, world, or universe, chances are the Millennial won't bother applying. Ryan Healy, in an article for www.EmployeeEvolution.com, writes: "The old approach is to list all of the responsibilities someone will have when they work for you. But we

Millennials aren't looking for a laundry list of things that you will tell us to do. We're looking for a reason to believe in your company. Give us one."[4] The rest of the job description should detail how the job will position Millennials for a successful career—and not just within the organization. In short, companies need to make a blatant appeal to Millennials' narcissistic streak and recognize that even in tough economic times, Millennials are not likely to settle for just any old job.

Boomer-friendly companies tell a different story in their job ads. They parade benefit programs, opportunities for career advancement, and the reputation of the company as enticements. They know that Boomers are staying in the workforce longer but want rich retirement plans and great health care.

A Lean Hiring Process

Millennials see no need for multiple callbacks and interviews; to them, this looks like disorganization. If a hiring decision takes months, Millennials fear that once on the inside they will suffer from a severe patience deficiency—a kind of corporate smoke inhalation that will take years off their lives. There is no need for a hiring decision to take months. Millennials don't wait for months.

As the authors of *Managing the Generation Mix* put it, Millennials demand "the immediate gratification of making an immediate impact by doing meaningful work immediately." Consider these two facts:

- 67.4 percent of Generation Y believes that one or two interviews at the most are acceptable.
- Only one in four Gen-Yers would consider staying five years at the same company.

Employers should act fast to stop top candidates from taking other jobs, as "[Millennials] need to have things right away can cause them to accept another job just down the street after applying with you."[5] Do the interview on the spot, as soon as the application is filled out. Check the references right away, and be prepared to offer the job the next day.[6]

FUSE TIP

If your system takes too long, take an ax to it. Cut the application cycle time in half—and then in half again.

Boomers, on the other hand, have far more patience. They know that their age may be a disadvantage and that, these days, companies have their pick of candidates. As long as they are still in the running, they will stay in the race. They will make their interests clear and follow up to see how the hiring process is progressing without becoming impatient. Are they throwing themselves at the job? Perhaps, but Boomers were taught that if you want something, you need to work hard to sell yourself.

Cool Coworkers Sell Companies

Millennials are people oriented. They get inspired when they get to meet the great people they will be working with. Hearing about the stellar career paths of people who started with the organization and got into excellent graduate schools, or who got great jobs internally or elsewhere, is proof to Millennials that they've found the right place. The best people for Millennials to connect with are other Millennials, who can let newbies in on how the job really works.

Boomers care about who they are working with, too, but they are less inclined to care about "cool" than they are to care about accomplishments. They want to work for someone they respect, someone they can learn from, someone they get along with well. After all, Boomers know that relationships make the corporate world go round.

Whether you're luring Boomer or Millennial, having a less-than-stellar team will not draw in new talent. As writer Penelope Trunk said in a blog post titled "Why You Should Never Complain About Your Company": "A former boss used to tell me that you should always hire A players because one B player brings everyone down—teams perform to their lowest performer. I think that's true. I also think that when an A sees a B on the team, the A doesn't want to come."[7]

The Choice Is Theirs

Millennials want to take a job because they *want* to, not because they *have* to. They hate being trapped in boring jobs or on a track they didn't choose. They need to be convinced that working for the organization is good for *anything* they want to do in the future. Even when the job market is tough, Millennials resist getting caught in a job they had to take out of necessity, as Shriram Harid notes in an article for *The Huffington Post*: "The recession has created a dismal employment picture for 18–29 year olds, the worst since 1972. But despite that harsh economic reality, today's 'Millennials' remain bizarrely rosy about their prospects."[8]

Boomers are less choosy, especially if they have lost a job and are trying to regain their economic footing. They have a practical view of work, and if the job pays well enough and gives them a meaningful way to use their skills, Boomers are likely to say yes.

Making Them Feel Special

Millennials expect personalization, to minimize the robotic feeling of the recruitment process. Because they have grown up in a highly customized culture where everything from learning plans to iTunes playlists to cancer treatments is individualized, they think recruitment should conform to their personal desires, as well. They think nothing of negotiating for interview times that work best for their schedules. They're surprised when they don't get a courtesy note thanking *them* for applying for a position. Millennials expect the company to know who they are and what they have to offer.

Boomers have an entirely different set of expectations. Taking a subservient attitude to the hiring manager and recruiter, they rearrange their priorities to make any interview time offered. After an interview, they send handwritten notes of appreciation the old-fashioned way—through the post office. Boomers focus on finding ways to stand out from the crowd by making their years of experience into compelling résumé reading.

The Promise of Intense, Meaningful Work

No organization can afford to waste resources on meaningless projects, and Millennials are especially sensitive to wasting time on trivial tasks. Every employee should be contributing from the get-go. Millennials love this. To them, it's cool to contribute to the organization's goals immediately; otherwise, they risk becoming a character from the movie *Office Space*.

Oftentimes, out of loyalty and the illusion of job security, Boomers stay at jobs that lack meaningful work. Those who have lost jobs and reentered the workforce have a heightened appreciation of what they most likely heard a bad boss say at some point in their career: "Just be thankful you have a job."

Access to Technology

Millennials use technology for everything. Technology is a universal language to them, part Esperanto, part mathematics, and part sign language. They learned it before they learned the sentence structure of their native tongue.

Most learned how to sign on to computer systems, to toggle views, to navigate user interfaces, and to move up in game levels before they could ride a tricycle.

Millennials are adept at all things technological. They have learned how to think like designers and programmers by being constant users. They are now experience-based learners. They are the Digital Natives described in Marc Prensky's groundbreaking work, *Digital Natives, Digital Immigrants*—they have never lived in a world without computers, cell phones, and iPods.[9] The *Sydney Morning Herald*'s Column 8 showed this to be exactly right: "During breakfast the other day, our six-year-old son, Lachlan, decided to make himself some toast. Grabbing a piece of bread, and on the point of placing it in the toaster, he said to his mother, 'Mum, how do I put the bread in—landscape or portrait?'"[10]

Boomers have mixed attitudes and skill levels when it comes to technology. Some are early adopters and embrace it wholeheartedly. Some still worry that the wrong keystroke will destroy their hard work. (How relieved they are to find the Undo key! Thanks, Microsoft!) These more reluctant Boomers would be wise and well-served to rely on their Millennial colleagues to teach them the technology ropes. Some Millennials may be patient enough to be great teachers; all will be extremely competent.

Retaining Boomers and Millennials

Once employees are in the door, it's important to keep them happy. As we've mentioned several times, turnover sucks a company's resources. Here are a few ways to make sure that Millennials in particular remain satisfied and motivated on the job.

Broadcasting Work

According to blogger wisdom, Millennials inherently follow the advice to "narrate your work." They use 2.0 tools—including blogs, "procial networks" such as Teambox that employ online collaboration tools, Tweets, and social networking—to broadcast not only the finished products of knowledge work but also the work in process. [11]

Millennials are more likely than other employees to talk publicly and broadcast digitally about the tasks and projects they're working on, the progress they're making, the resources they're finding particularly helpful, and the questions, roadblocks, and challenges that come up. Employers should support and encourage this sharing of information because the narration becomes part of the digital record of the organization, which means that it becomes searchable, findable, and "reference-able." It also results in synergy and new ideas, as people throughout the organization and across disciplines become aware of what is being worked on.

Millennials know that narrating their work, when done right, saves time, increases productivity, gets better results, and knits the organization together more tightly. Boomers, used to working in silos, are more likely to see work narration as a narcissistic waste of time. Employers should encourage Boomers to find their voices, too, and to consider this very twenty-first-century approach to information-sharing as a possible best practice.

No BS

Millennials have radar detectors that can immediately spot BS. They'll know it if you shine them on. And they'll leave you at the door. Boomers take schmoozing as corporate foreplay, and they are more likely to grin and bear it. Lack of authenticity is not a deal-killer to them.

Show EQ (Emotional IQ)

Millennials want an emotional connection to their employer, their work, and their colleagues. Millennial-friendly companies are empathetic. They focus on getting Millennials to care about their organizations by showing that they care about Millennials. This is important because, coming from a child-centric culture, Millennials have been asked how they *feel* about every aspect of their lives since being gently removed from their mothers' wombs by prescheduled cesarean sections. They were not asked to suck it up when they lost, told that it's just life when things didn't always go their way, or sent to their rooms without dinner when they acted up. Instead, they were encouraged to express their feelings and were counseled by parents, teachers, coaches, and therapists. Most of their interactions have been mediated. Try to find a Millennial who has settled an argument by a fistfight, or handled a disagreement with a teacher without some parent intervention. Their feelings matter.

During the recruitment process, savvy employers meet this expectation by establishing rapport and inquiring about the applicant's interests outside of the job. Expert advice urges employers to "stress the qualitative aspects of the company, its mission, and any community work it does. Do some empathetic listening to your Millennial candidates, repeating their key points so that they know that you have heard them."[12]

A great deal of current research shows that Millennials have greater emotional intelligence (EQ) than do adults in other generations. EQ is the essence of social media. Boomers have plenty of EQ too; they've just never been encouraged to show it or share it. The best leaders have always had high EQ: perceiving, assessing, and managing emotions—their own and others'. It's been called people sense or intuition or how to make friends and influence people. According to John P. Kotter of Harvard Business School, "Difficult-to-manage relationships sabotage more business than anything else—it is not a question of strategy that gets us into trouble; it is a question of emotions." What are the implications of developing EQ? Better opportunity for

Boomers and Millennials to play well together in the corporate sandbox.[13]

Making a Difference in the World

Millennial workers are looking to have a positive impact on the world through what they do at work. They are looking for a chance to help a company go green, to contribute to philanthropies, to help children and the elderly and those in need—anywhere in the world.

Ask them what causes they care about and where they heard or read about them. Ask for their ideas on how to build a "communications and community" ethos in the organization. They are acutely aware that they are inheriting a deeply flawed world, with its problems of overpopulation, climate change, pollution, financial collapse, terrorism, energy and food shortages, and many other ills. This is an area where it particularly behooves Boomers to show they really do care about helping the next generations face threatening conditions that the Boomers themselves contributed to, and Boomers can model the activism that changed the world for their generation.

FUSE TIP

Social good is Millennial Red Bull. Allowing time to give back is energizing and builds loyalty to your company and brand.

Don't forget, Millennials have been raised by Boomers—the generation that brought the civil rights movement, ended a war, and initiated modern environmentalism. Give both your Boomer and Millennial employees a chance at activities that make a difference. Awareness of action taken on social and environmental causes travels fast. Causes are a perfect way to find common ground and build rapport and trust that can enhance working relationships. The entire organization can become cause oriented, building connections, community, and brand.

FUSE FACTOIDS

From the Pew Research Center:

- Nine out of ten Millennials believe they'll have enough money to lead the kind of life they want.

From the Bureau of Labor Statistics:

- Thirty-seven percent of all Millennials are either unemployed or out of the work force.
- Thirty-six percent of all eighteen- to twenty-nine-year-olds depend on their parents for financial assistance.

For eighteen- to twenty-four-year-olds, it's 50 percent. "Indeed, one-in-six older Millennials, age twenty-two and older, has boomeranged back to a parent's home on account of the recession."[14]

Finding Your Next Opportunity

Whether you are a Millennial or a Boomer, if you're looking for work, you'll want to get out in the job search traffic. Today, that's as much of a digital experience as it is an exercise in effective in-person networking and conversations. When it comes to finding work, the power of "who you know" still reigns. But now there are new ways to get to know the right people.

Online Recruiting

Newspaper ads are no longer the place to look for meaningful work opportunities. Advertisers of all kinds have fled to media that have larger key audiences. This is especially true of job recruiting, where huge Internet-based networks such as www.Craigslist.com, www.Monster.com, and www.CareerBuilder.com have ruled. More focused sites include www.Indeed.com, and the hottest trend is in venture capital–sponsored sites, where jobs are posted for their portfolio companies, such as www.usv.com/jobs.

There are also specialty online recruitment sites for almost every industry, such as www.AttorneyRecruitingSpecialists.com

for lawyers, as well as specialty sites focused on income, such as www.TheLadders.com, which advertises only jobs paying more than $100,000 a year.

FUSE TIP

Pick a hip venue for a recruiting event. Have video games and the latest technology available. Get a local media celebrity or DJ to MC and entertain. Have really great food. Let Millennials see that you get their definition of fun.

Entire business models are built on online recruiting—through local, national, and trade-related websites. At the macro level, www.Onrec.com, the website of *Online Recruitment* magazine, has the largest directory of online recruitment sites in the world. The Internet Recruiting Resource Center (available at www.RecruitersNetwork.com/resources) and www.Business.com have hundreds of online resources that are free for employers, including quick tips, how-to articles, and videos. (You do know what résumé spiders and robots are, don't you?) And of course there are literally thousands of blogs dealing with recruitment, some of the best of which are listed in David Hakala's article, "10 Must-Read Online Recruiting Blogs" for www.HRWorld.com.[15]

Social Networking Websites

If you are like the majority of Millennials, you're applying for jobs online. Your first stops will probably be Facebook, LinkedIn, and www.simplyhired.com. There you'll find companies that know they need to create social media accounts as part of their recruiting strategy, and are leveraging social networks to do it.

FUSE TIP

Smart companies assign Millennial employees to make their presence known in the social media sphere. They constantly update social networking sites with what's hot in the organization and what socially responsible issues the company cares about.

For Boomers, the most comfortable place for online job hunting is LinkedIn, which describes itself as the world's largest professional networking site, with more than 100 million users representing 150 industries around the world. LinkedIn is leveraging the power of its network with a search capability that enables subscribing companies to find people with specific expertise by geography. Its goal is to replace the executive recruiting industry. Finding people you know with connections you want to make is the beauty of this site. Your contacts can introduce you to theirs, and open doors with the click of a mouse.

Corporate Website Job Boards

Most organizations know by now that they need to have an online presence and that their website must have a career or jobs area. From Google to GoDaddy, the sites geared toward Millennials are cool, interactive, and tech-oriented. Companies today use banners that showcase their employee benefits, or they place recruiting banners in blogs that Millennials frequent. Best Buy has Internet-based job application kiosks in key locations, both because customers will presumably be familiar with the company's philosophy and service and also because of the convenience factor. The strategy is working: hiring at these locations is robust, and turnover has decreased.

Boomers also rely on websites to get to really know a company. That includes a thorough review of key benefit programs for healthcare and retirement. Boomers do their homework. They use the Internet to prepare impressive questions for their interviews.

Personal Networks

You are your own best recruiter. Use your network of friends, neighbors, family members, colleagues, vendors, and acquaintances to find job prospects. Savvy HR people and managers are asking Millennials they already know if they have friends who fit their job requirements. They are networking within personal networks using Facebook company career pages.

Millennials and Boomers alike would be wise to see each other as job-hunting resources. So instead of cringing the next time you see your parents' friends and they tell you how much you've grown, view them as a conduit to your next job. Likewise, don't be surprised if your parents' or grandparents' Boomer friends hear that you've landed in a great company and come to you sharing their career aspirations and qualifications, and inquiring about possible openings.

Finding a job and keeping it are universal concerns, whether you're a Boomer or a Millennial. What differs among the working generations is how you go about looking for work; whether you understand how digital and yet personally networked the world is; and your motivational profiles, especially in regard to EQ, using technology, and social causes. We loved this comment from a Millennial on Chester Evan's former blog: "To people my age, entering the workforce is like landing on the beaches of Normandy." Surely, both generations can understand that!

CHAPTER 2 **FUSIONS**

- Seek companies that understand, accept, and mirror your key needs and tell you so in their recruitment campaigns.
- Online job hunting is here to stay. It brings a jackpot of choices if you mine your networks and know where to search.
- Employees are a reflection of a company and its culture. Get to know some during the interview process to see if it's the right place for you.
- Open information-sharing and blogging has a productivity payoff. It's natural for Millennials to document their work. Boomers would be wise to do the same.
- Emotional intelligence is key whether you're hiring or being hired. Companies want to know whether potential hires can get along in the workplace, and employees want to know that their emotional well-being will be addressed.

CHAPTER 3

What's Love Got to Do with It?

"When the rate of change inside an institution becomes slower than the rate of change outside, the end is in sight. The only question is when."
—Jack Welch, former CEO, General Electric

Does your employer get you excited about what you do and motivate you to do it well? Is motivation even on employers' radar screens?

It should be, especially to keep young workers happy. As Barbara Dwyer, CEO of The Job Journey, says: "This [Millennial] generation is going to come to work with higher expectations than any other. They will be quickly disappointed if it's not as good as they had hoped. With one click of a mouse, they can tell thousands of other people, 'Don't come to work for XYZ company.'"[1]

The average Millennial works just six hours per day. They have a job satisfaction rate of 20 percent and stick with the same job for an average of only two years. Says a twenty-eight-year-old quoted in a *Fortune* magazine article, "If we don't like a job, we quit."[2]

Recruitment isn't enough to be successful; employers have to work at keeping Millennials interested and inspired. The key is to find ways to leverage their unique talents to the benefit of your organization.

The crux of motivating and retaining Millennials is to understand how they view the world and their role in an organization. If the right moves have been made in recruiting them, the organization is well on its way to understanding what they want from an employer. Millennials do not leave jobs because there is a compelling reason to leave but because there is *no compelling reason to stay*. They leave jobs because the work is not challenging and/or rewarding. They stay with organizations that promote their professional growth and provide personal satisfaction through respect, recognition, and reward.

Harvard Business School professor James Heskett explains that Millennials are focused inward, on their personal development: "They want an accelerated path to success, often exaggerate the impact of their own contributions, are not willing 'to pay the price,' and have little fear of authority." He goes on to conclude that Millennials are not always good candidates for long-term employment, because they will quickly seek other jobs—or leisure—instead of staying in a job where they are not personally developing.[3]

FUSE TIP

Rock climbers don't go straight up. Careers are built by reaching another foothold, gaining a fresh perspective, and preparing for the next move. Make sure the Millennials at your company are given opportunities to grow and to take on new challenges.

There are many ways to motivate and retain Millennials, and they can be mixed and matched to create a more stimulating and rewarding work environment. Here are a baker's dozen of the top motivators, in order of importance to Millennials. We start with Money/Benefits, because it is the foundation of employment. However, as we explain in subsequent chapters, many Millennials are not motivated primarily by money, or they are motivated differently than other generations. We also cover salary and benefits/rewards in chapters 4 and 5.

- Money/Benefits
- Work/Life Balance
- Interesting Work
- Social Causes
- Sociable Environment
- Respect and Appreciation

- Flexible Scheduling
- Mentors and Managers
- Access to Latest Technology
- Continual Learning
- Continual Performance Reviews/Feedback
- EQ Environment
- Little Things

Let's now take a closer look at these motivators one by one.

Money/Benefits

Everyone works for money, no matter how idealistic they are, and this includes Millennials.

Because these employees are young and inexperienced, some managers are tempted to pay them as little as possible. That is an excellent strategy if you enjoy high turnover. Millennials know how to get data and can easily compare their pay with salary ranges for their job type.

Employers can access salary data themselves to make sure their offers are competitive. Counsels Peter Sheahan, in an article titled "What Millennial Workers Want": "Ensure that the compensation your company offers is slightly above the average for your industry and region. Rather than offering a low starting salary with the possibility of a raise or bonus in six months, make [Millennials] an up-front offer they can't refuse."[4]

In addition, make sure the offer will hold up in the long term. Don't offer a higher starting salary knowing that promises of raises and promotions may never materialize, or that the employee may not be around to collect!

Annual raises of 2 to 3 percent using traditional pay-for-performance charts will neither motivate nor retain young workers, as we explain in chapter 4. We are strong advocates of pay for potential and incentive compensation. Millennials rarely have a long-term perspective, so consider awarding quarterly bonuses instead of, or in addition to, annual bonuses. Change long-term compensation incentive plans so that payoffs take effect after shorter time periods.

For optimal motivation, a smorgasbord of benefits should complement salary, as detailed in chapter 5. Millennials value traditional as well as customized, nontraditional benefits. Provide longer vacations after shorter lengths of service; most Millennials get bored easily with routine and value time to decompress. Above all, *ask them* what benefits and policies they would value.

Work/Life Balance

Our favorite summation of a generation's attitude toward jobs: "When I signed on here, I never figured you were going to make me work the whole time!"[5] Finding work/life balance is a major quest for Millennials, who like to work hard but require lives of their own. Employment is a major part of their week, but it is not their life. It provides the funds to fuel their life. A career that allows them the opportunity to continue the other aspects of their existence—educational, social, spiritual, or entrepreneurial—is highly attractive. The employer that finds a way to offer this authentically—not just giving it lip service—will garner loyalty and longevity.

FUSE TIP

No Millennial worth employing will stick around without being allowed to have work/life balance. Even Boomers will move heaven and earth for an employer that supports it. Balance is priceless. Supporting balance doesn't mean you say "yes" to every request for flexibility, though. Balance the needs of the business with the needs of the employee.

Boomers also are seeking the holy grail of balance. They've been acculturated to "whoever works the longest hours wins." With slumped shoulders and increasingly dour faces, they grind on and seek long-term balance in the fantasized land of retirement. Given Millennials' advocacy on this point, though, we're seeing more Boomers take a stand in favor of enjoying some daylight hours NOW. They don't want to miss their kids' or grandkids' sports events or dance recitals, and many are taking on athletic and community activities after normal working hours. We've heard no reports of productivity declining from making *carpe diem* their motto. The voices from both ends of the age spectrum are persuading many employers to accommodate personal schedules.

Interesting Work

We all need meaningful work. Through thousands of one-on-one interactions, researchers at the Institute for Labor and Mental Health found that socially meaningless work is a major cause of stress, and that "most people have a real need for meaning and purpose in their lives . . . that transcends the competitive marketplace."[6]

For Millennials, that need is acute. Connecting work to meaning through discussion, examples, and pay-it-forward thinking creates an emotional connection with an organization that benefits both parties.

Millennials are a DIY generation. Schooled by gamer technology, they operate at twitch speed and learn by doing, through trial and error. Change is the air they breathe. So, giving them work that involves variety, challenge, flexibility, and opportunity for advancement is crucial. They want to learn, and they like to participate in projects that give them hands-on experience. Their interest lies in making significant contributions to organizations as they learn, not in waiting for someone else to decide it's time to be seen and heard.

To really prime motivation, involve Millennials in direct contact with internal and external customers so they better understand *why* their jobs are important and what's in it for *them*. For extra points, you can emulate Google, embracing creativity and innovation by allowing employees one day a week just to come up with new product ideas.

Social Causes

Research suggests that Millennials want to work for organizations that are civic-minded and socially responsible. These organizations make good products or services, give back to the community, and are good stewards of the environment. www.Beyond.com, a network of niche career communities, suggests that employers establish a community service program that fits the company culture and communicate it to employees via the company's website, job ads, interviews, and corporate collateral.[7] The companies that do this heighten their profile and perceived worth as employers.

Sociable Environment

In his paper "The ABC of XYZ," Mark McCrindle speculates that high parental divorce rates and having two working parents may have caused Millennials to be more peer-oriented and more inclined to place a premium on workplace culture than other generations do. They want an environment where they can interact socially, work collaboratively, and enjoy being friends with coworkers. Creating office space that encourages coworkers to share ideas and interact with one another can promote this sociability and teamwork. This generation wants to look forward to going to work every day and wants to enjoy a fun, friendly, and creative environment in which to work and grow as individuals—and as collaborators.

FUSE TIP

Provide the simple pleasures. Invest in a Wii or a Ping-Pong table. Open a coffee shop or café instead of a break room and watch your employee satisfaction scores climb.

Respect and Appreciation

Those who study the Cogenerational Workplace™ seem to agree that respect and appreciation of Millennials' ideas and work is a key motivator and retention factor. The more their work is shown to be key to the resolution of a problem, the retention of key customers, the development of a new product line, or the overall success of your organization, the more likely the work will motivate them and cause them to stay the course.

Millennials look for rewarding opportunities. There is never too much public praise, too many thank-you notes, face-to-face thank-yous, and small rewards from managers, especially if these rewards recognize accomplishments as they are made. The world for Millennials has become incentivized. Customer loyalty is bought with frequent buyer programs, points, or discounts. So is employee loyalty.

FUSE TIP

Instant gratification keeps on giving. Stock up on movie tickets, Peet's Coffee gift cards, and other small tokens of appreciation. Give them out the minute you see Millennials doing something noteworthy.

Flexible Scheduling

Millennials are productivity machines. They will figure out how to get as much done in six to seven hours as the average Boomer does in eight to ten. We suggest that you let them. Should employers limit their workday or let them off early? Maybe—if they're getting the work done, it's worth consideration.

It's the employers that offer work-schedule flexibility such as summer hours, flextime, or work-at-home programs that will top the motivational top-ten list. This obviously has to be done in a way that is fair to all employees, and assigned work must get done on deadline. But our feedback is that employers with robust flextime programs generally see greater productivity because of the greater motivation and appreciation of their staff members.

Mentors and Managers

Mentors are crucial to the success of Millennials. The upcoming generations have been coached their entire lives, from preschool through college. And, because Millennials are by definition new to the professional workplace, they need mentoring, no matter how smart and confident they seem.

FUSE TIP

Mentor early and often. Connect the Millennial employees with a mentor *before* they begin work and ensure that they stay close for the crucial first hundred days.

If you're mentoring a Millennial, remember that affirmation and specific suggestions work best. Instead of asking broad questions such as "How's it going?" let them know that what they do is important. Discuss concrete action steps they can take toward their goals, and offer resources and information to help them on their way. Share your own stories. The goal of mentoring is to create future leaders who don't make the same mistakes you did. Resist the temptation to parent—no matter how much Millennial men and women remind you of your own flesh and blood. Because they work so well in team situations, consider mentoring Millennials in groups so they can act as each other's resources or peer mentors. Talk to them about the business and how it makes money. Talk to them about how the company does good or improves the community.

Remember that mentoring isn't a one-way process. Marc Prenksy recounts the story of the reverse mentoring Jack Welch did at GE. Just before he left, Welch had his top thousand managers mentored by young workers. They may have been new to GE, but they understood the newest technologies better than the old-timers. So, too, Prensky notes, "Microsoft now sees the role of its managers as 'clearing obstacles from the paths' chosen by its programmers, often its youngest employees, who carry the firm's future products in their heads."[8]

Leading, especially for these gamers, means giving explicit instructions, continuous assessments, and constant feedback. Millennials thrive on instant gratification and frequent rewards. Communicate clear goals and expectations, then back off. Let them do projects their way so long as results are delivered your way.

Access to Latest Technology

Almost every business decision is informed by rapid changes in technology. When they have the latest technology, Millennials can have the greatest impact on customers and the bottom line. Marc Prensky covers this point best: "Digital Natives are used to receiving information really fast. They like to parallel process and multitask. They prefer their graphics before their text rather than the opposite. They prefer random access (like hypertext). They function best when networked."[9] Elsewhere he writes, "Their online life has become an entire strategy for how to live, survive, and thrive in the twenty-first century, where cyberspace is a part of everyday life."[10]

To keep Millennials engaged, they need to have the right tech tools to do their jobs. Think every imaginable technology: podcasts, vlogs and blogs, online brainstorming sessions, gaming and productivity software, and flexible hardware with graphics card, unlimited bandwidth and RAM, and the processors and servers to dish them up. The focus is on speed, customization, and interactivity. No one can see the future, but Millennials know where it is and how to get there through technology.

Continual Learning

Millennials are passionate about lifelong education and require ongoing training. They know that the key to remaining relevant is continual learning. In a survey from McCrindle Research, 79.8 percent of Millennials polled said that career development through additional training was very important to them. Nearly 90 percent agreed that regular training from their employer would motivate them to stay with an organization longer. Overall, they preferred "soft skills" (communication and interaction) as opposed to "hard skills" (technical training), which was seen as relevant only for a current job.

Be aware that Millennials will not read traditional written, static information for skills training or career development. Some organizations, especially high-tech companies such as Sun Microsystems and Google, have recognized this and developed interactive electronic instruction. Companies with large numbers of blue-collar Millennials have successfully implemented hands-on electronic instruction. UPS and—yes—the U.S. Army are leaders in this area.

The most desirable employers make sure there are opportunities to learn in a variety of media—online, via podcasts and thumb drives, over lunch-and-learns, from webinars, in classes, in customized role-playing video games, and from varied work experiences. Individual customization is key, as it is in coaching, mentoring, and job rotations. Some organizations also offer strength and personality assessments that enhance self-awareness among employees.

We are often asked why organizations should spend money on training if Millennials are just going to leave anyway. The answer is that if training is offered, Millennials will appreciate the organization and have a higher probability of becoming intrapreneurs who will run new business lines ten to twenty years down the road.

In addition, employees are customers, too, and will remember the positive experiences they had while working for an organization that cared enough to invest in their development—even if they were there for only a short time. After they leave, they could come back to do business with you. Before its collapse, Arthur Andersen had it right: Its recruiting material explicitly expected new hires to be with the firm for only two years, but promised it would be the best postgraduate education they could ever get! Many Arthur grads went on to be CFOs and CEOs of other companies—and turned around and worked with Arthur when they had the power to make the engagement decisions.

Continual Performance Reviews/Feedback

Millennials want constant feedback. As one put it: "If we're only at a company for two years, we cannot wait for our one-year review to find out how we're doing. [We] will invent the on-the-spot performance review. Spot reviews lead to consistent improvement, and consistent improvement is what truly matters to [us]."[11] Whether you can stomach giving constant feedback or not, allow Millennials to request a performance review at any time during their first ninety days on the job.

In fact, this may be a good idea for Boomers too! Some of them (usually those who are feeling vulnerable because of the current economic uncertainty) want more feedback than they are used to getting.

Establishing a clear career track, supported by a performance-review process, helps all employees understand how they're doing and encourages them to keep improving and moving forward, whether they're with you for the long- or short-term tenure. Sounds simple, right? It is. But it is being done very poorly in many organizations.

EQ Environment

As we detailed in chapter two, Millennials are more psychologically forthright, adept, empathic, and emotionally demanding than other generations. As McCrindle researchers put it, "For the twenty-first-century generations, educational and technological developments have had psychological impacts. We are dealing with [Millennials] today who need to be engaged more on the emotive scale than the cognitive scale. . . . the shift in focus from IQ (intellectual intelligence) to EQ (emotional intelligence)."[12]

What this means to their employers is that Millennials demand emotional validation in the workplace; heart stuff, not just head stuff. Managers need to connect on a nonintellectual plane, inquiring about Millennials' well-being and how they feel about their work. They have to manage people, not jobs.

Little Things

Beyond these top motivators, it's the small things that can convince Millennials to play and to stay. Here are a few suggestions:

- Make their first day unforgettable.
- Celebrate employee birthdays.
- Give them business cards immediately.
- Let them attend management meetings.
- Create mentoring, reverse-mentoring, and social activities.
- Create a network of peers, mentors, and senior staff from the moment they cross the threshold.
- Set up office spaces to encourage social interaction and exchange of ideas.
- Assign workstations closer to more senior employees.
- Hold only productive meetings.

Motivation is as complex—or simple—as you want to make it. It starts with understanding the psychological profile of your workers and, to do it right, requires that you customize incentives, keeping an eye out for fairness among all employee cohorts. Money is always a motivator. But especially for Millennials, instant and continuous small rewards, praise, recognition, and time off are terrific incentives.

CHAPTER 3 **FUSIONS**

- Millennials leave jobs not because there is a compelling reason to leave but because there is no compelling reason to stay.
- To motivate them, you need to meet their psychological needs for frequent rewards and praise and give them more frequent time off.
- Meaningless work is a major cause of stress, especially for Millennials. Connect work to meaning.
- Millennials demand continual training opportunities. Accessible training likely will result in "stickiness"—their becoming intrapreneurs who will run your business ten to twenty years down the road.

- Millennials are more psychological than other generations. They need to be engaged on the emotive scale more than the cognitive scale. They are forcing managers to manage people, not jobs.

CHAPTER 4

Show Me the Money

"Money was never a big motivation for me, except as a way to keep score. The real excitement is playing the game."
—Donald Trump

"For Baby Boomers, the workplace competition was about money, and the material things that represent one's earnings . . . But [Millennials] see the competition as about fulfillment, and they are determined to get it."
—Penelope Trunk[1]

These two viewpoints cover the range of opinion, information, and misinformation about compensation. Despite The Donald's proclamation (said when he already had billions), our opinion is that we all work for money. No matter what else lures us into the workplace, no matter how our souls are salved by good deeds, our egos massaged by visible praise, our need for companionship met by fellow toilers, it is lucre that forces us away from World of Warcraft, YouTube, the Shopping Channel, Facebook, and filling our 160-gig iPods with more Metallica, and makes us go into the office.

If you won the lottery tomorrow, would you go back to your day job? We always ask this question at some point in our presentations. Even the rare priest in the audience has looked thoughtful while contemplating the answer. The rest of us mere mortals say they'd quit in a New York minute if the financial necessity of working were eliminated. This holds true from geezers to Millennials.

But the importance of money is a matter of degree. To many Boomers, including an author of this book, money paid the expenses in our single-earner family; it served as a measuring stick that showed us how we were performing in relation to our peers; it paved the way in our lockstep promotions; and it is absolutely necessary to funding our retirement. There weren't other types of compensation. Millennials, on the other hand, tend to think of pay as a naturally occurring, immediate, direct result of appreciated individual work. They see it as an immediate effect of their work, and there is little expectation of and little patience for long-term incremental rewards.

The 411 on Millennial Financials

Although they are often said to eschew monetary rewards, and have a great eagerness for rewards outside the monetary pay scale, many Millennials find their financial reality daunting.

- Many Millennials are operating under crushing debt: Most college students graduate with close to $20,000 in student loan debt. Graduate and professional students easily can incur $100,000 in loans that have to be repaid as of day one on the job. These knowledge economy workers have made a great investment in higher education, where costs have multiplied by triple digits at both private and public colleges in the last decade and a half.[2] And they're still escalating.
- Millennials now entering the workplace earn less than previous generations. Most workers' real wages have been stagnant since the turn of the twenty-first century, and the gap between productivity growth and workers' wages is at a historically high level. The inflation-adjusted earnings of new college grads have fallen dramatically.
- Millennials' entry into the workforce has coincided with rapid increases in key living costs. Education, housing, and healthcare costs have increased rapidly over the last decade. Rents have gone up 50 percent in major metropolitan areas in the last ten years. Even with home prices falling in many regions as a result of the mortgage crisis, median home prices have skyrocketed in geographically appealing areas

across the country, severely limiting affordability for first-time buyers.[3]

- Millennials are paying more into Social Security than they pay in income taxes, even though most expect Social Security to be dried up long before they reach retirement age.

It's clear from these numbers that many Millennials are under increasing financial stress. Consequently, salary will be very important to them. In fact, while Boomers are more likely to want to be paid through a combination of salary and long-term savings and retirement options, Millennials generally tend to prefer to receive immediate compensation for their work.

Because of the drastic economic reversals they've seen in the business world, Millennials are cautious, thinking that neither they nor their organizations will be around long enough to reap the rewards of a pension plan or long-term savings options. They want a check and portable 401(k) match to make their own retirement and investment decisions.

How does Millennial financial stress play out in real dollar terms in today's workplace? Let's take a look at determining salary basics. The questions are: What's a job worth to you? And what are you worth to your potential employer? The first thing to do is understand your organization's total compensation system, including its compensation philosophy—pay for performance or pay for potential, discussed below—and its attitude toward incentives and benefits, discussed in chapters 3 and 5.

Compensation Philosophy: Pay for Performance vs. Pay for Potential

Pay for performance is the compensation system the Boomers typically use to set and increase pay. It's what most of us who've been working for a while are used to: salaries increase slowly and steadily the more you work, and we do mean slowly—the average salary increase is 3 percent annually. Seriously.

Why Pay for Performance Doesn't Work: The Merit Increase Matrix Game

Ever wonder on what basis your salary increases (or doesn't increase) over time? How decisions are made about your pay? Has your company said they pay you for your performance? Or that they reward for results?

Here's the way it really works in many companies today.

First, let's address performance. Your organization may have a rating system to determine if you are meeting expectations: good, great, fantastic, wonderful, outstanding, walking on water—or not meeting expectations: needing improvement, one foot out the door, they wish you were gone.

No matter how the rating scale is presented, here are the basics: 80 percent of employees are rated as doing okay, being cool, getting it done. Forget the labels of good to great; in truth, only 10 to 15 percent of you will be in the "star" category, and 5 to 10 percent may be in the "cull the herd" (get 'em out the door) category. The 80 percent of you in the middle are often divided into three or four categories that are shades of gray in which the distinctions of why you are pretty good, good, or really good are very hard to find.

Now let's tie that to your pay increase. Your organization has only so much money that management wants to spend on pay increases. This is called a salary increase or merit increase budget. Their job is to figure out how to lay that money on you and all of your colleagues. In their search for a solution, they develop a table that will tell your bosses what they are allowed to give you if you meet certain performance standards, measured on an organization-wide rating scale. This is referred to as a salary increase or merit increase matrix, or guide chart.

This chart quantifies your performance level and sometimes your length of service with the organization and/or your position in a salary range, and gives salary increase guidelines to your manager. It is linked to the increase budget, which for the past twenty years has been 4 percent (plus or minus 2 percent, depending on the year). During the past two years, it has been down around 2 percent (for those organizations that actually gave increases), and in the great boom of the late 1990s was as high as 5 to 6 percent in certain industries and for hard-to-find positions.

Assuming 4 percent as a budget, here is the typical merit increase matrix for a company:

PERFORMANCE DESCRIPTION	%	COMMENTS
Phenomenal	6%	Walks on water—10 percent of you
Fantastic	5%	A star in the making—10 percent of you
You Rock	4%	Doing good—60 percent of you
You Almost Rock	3%	A little extra effort, and you too can be a star—10 percent of you
Not Cutting It (Yet)	2%	Can't give you zero . . . feeling guilty—5 percent of you
Not!	0%	Okay, you're gone—5 percent of you

That middle group—Fantastic, You Rock, and You Almost Rock—makes up 80 percent of the population of your organization. With a 1 percent difference in your salary increase between the categories, let's do the math.

Pay for performance = a six-pack of beer. If you are making what the average worker makes ($47,569.60 per year[4], a 1 percent difference in your pay is $475.70 per year, $18.30 gross per pay period (if you have twenty-six pay periods per year), and about $12.81 net per pay period after Social Security, Medicare, and federal, state, and other taxes. That's about $6.40 per week. And according to our research, that's what you'd pay for a six-pack of beer. Or—if you are lucky, and you are bumped up a level—two six-packs!

You can't *really* believe that this nominal differentiation in pay is motivational and drives performance results.

It doesn't. In fact, it may aggravate working relationships for folks who believe that their performance really matters in determining their future value and find that where the rubber meets the road—their pay—it makes no difference.

Why Pay for Potential Does Work

Pay for potential is a compensation philosophy that tries to level the playing field based on what each employee brings to the job and how well he leverages those competencies. It's a new concept that gets rid of "the more years you work, the more money you should make" mentality, and recognizes individual talent and potential. While it is challenging for the Boomers to accept a new way of thinking about compensation, pay for potential is far and away the best plan to connect and engage with Millennials.

Here's how it works.

Say you've been writing computer programs since you were twelve and have a few video games that you've created as well. Why are you being paid less than a person who has ten fewer years of real-world experience than you do even if you are younger? Because your talent and potential do not count in the twentieth-century workplace until you demonstrate them through performance. If your organization has moved into the twenty-first century and believes in pay for potential—rewarding you for the skills and competencies you bring in and how those unique assets get manifested in your work regardless of your age or years of workplace experience—then your salary may actually reflect your true gifts.

One way to assess and integrate pay for potential is by using a "nine box system," which allows organizations to blend the best of both pay philosophies. With potential rated low to high on an X axis and performance rated low to high on a Y axis, it shows steady performers, potential stars, and rock stars as categories of potential. Potential is assessed in terms of "how high" (next level, top management, etc.) and "how soon" (readiness).

So, imagine that you are an entry-level whiz kid—all the potential in the world, but still developing. Traditional salary increase programs in most companies will make you earn your spurs in time spent on the job before you start racking up the big bucks. Why? It's a way that compensation planners "manage" your expectations and keep you in line. And opportunities for promotion are limited since many companies suffer from middle-management malaise, having eliminated these positions in cost-cutting measures (or in response to a fading management fad du jour known as "increased span of control").

This is frustrating. It is why many money-motivated Millennials (and they do exist) will bolt to new opportunities as soon as the great recession of 2007–20?? eases up. Unless you happen to be in one of those organizations that recognizes your potential. What these companies have done is break the mold. They will accelerate your compensation not just based on your performance but on what you bring to the table, namely, an asset they want to secure for the long-run. It may be your intellect, your inventiveness, your ingenuity, your incessant drive. But they love you and want to keep you.

Here is how it works.

Normally, your performance is the only driver of pay. In a nine-box system that recognizes multiple dimensions (see diagram below), the actual increases will be higher for those with comparable performance whose potential is far superior.

% INCREASE	POTENTIAL		
PERFORMANCE	GOOD	GREAT	ROCK STAR
Superior	6	10	15
Exceeds	4	6	10
Meets	2	4	6

As you can see, the “good” potential performer could expect to receive merit increases of 2–6 percent based on “traditional” pay-for-performance programs. This is about the limit in most old-school compensation systems. Not Exciting? But, in this example, under a pay-for-*potential* system, the rock star with superior performance could receive a 15 percent increase. This is epic.

Find a company that innovates in its approach to compensation—that is, it recognizes and accelerates pay for those whose potential exceeds their age—and you may decide to stay for a while!

Getting the Salary You Want

Before you can develop an idea of what you should be getting paid, you need to do some market research. These three sites will give you an idea of what a person in your region, in your industry, and with your job title might make:

- www.Salary.com (A great site, although pay scales tend to be high.)
- www.PayScale.com (A dynamic site that relies on people submitting their own job profiles and salary data.)
- www.Glassdoor.com (A snarky website for dishing the 411 on companies, that also provides compensation information.)

You should also understand that all components of pay are negotiable and that *you are the chief negotiator*. Think of it as free agency. How do you think A-Rod got his record-breaking salary?

When you go into a job interview and you're asked what salary range you have in mind, *do not answer*. Ask nicely to defer the answer until you've discussed the job a bit more. Let the interviewer suggest a figure. Nod wisely. Do not snap at that lure like a hungry bass. Tell the interviewer your research has shown the range for the job to be whatever it is, and that you believe your experience qualifies you to come in at the top of that range. You won't get it, but you'll probably get a counteroffer somewhere in between.

Or maybe you're already parked in a cube, wondering whether you can sleep there if your paycheck doesn't cover the rent. Do you believe your work is worth more money than you're making? If so, you've got company. According to a recent www.Salary.com survey, of 7,141 individuals and 363 human resource or other company representatives, 65 percent of respondents said they're looking for a new job within the next three months. Fifty-six percent of those say they're looking because they believe they are underpaid.

Again, do the market research on comparable jobs in your region.

Additionally, the HR department may have a regional salary range book. Ask if you can see this; it will be more accurate regarding what employees in your region make than the employer surveys conducted by the big websites—such as the ones mentioned above. Bigger organizations and public entities publish their pay ranges for all jobs. Ask![5]

FUSE TIP

Open the curtain on pay practices. Suspicious minds are quick to distrust their leaders when pay information is kept secret. Being transparent will pay off, provided you administer your pay plans with consistency. Take the mystery out of the numbers.

Assessing a Compensation Package

As you begin mulling over the total value of an employer's compensation package, start by figuring out the organization's compensation philosophy. Do they want to motivate you to perform, or just pay you for showing up? Or are they trying to get you to work your buns off for as cheap as they can get away with, knowing that right before you leave, you'll sound off about pay and they can adjust your salary a little then? Know their MO (modus operandi)—before and after you join them. Once you've assessed the compensation dynamic, move on to the following areas.

Paying the Bills

How much do they offer you for the basics—showing up, doing your job, producing some results? This is your base salary. The HR department will spend a lot of time comparing your job to other jobs and trying to figure out what you are worth in the marketplace. The truth is, there is a lot of variability in the market depending on location, supply and demand, and the skill set required. The more skills you have, the more you should get paid. But pay is an art form—not a science. Translation? You have plenty of room to negotiate—if you are good.

Understand that your initial base salary is what *all* your future raises and salaries will key off of. Pay attention to this, as the money you earn—lifetime earnings, Social Security payouts, and benefits, including retirement contributions—is cumulative. Throughout your working years, you've got to keep leveraging your salary, moving it up at every opportunity.

Pay Raises

Compensation experts will tell you that pay raises depend on

- Your industry
- The market and market pay for your job in your region
- The pay practices of your organization
- Your performance on the job

All of that is true. What is also true is that there are some *cheats*—just as in any game—to help you get raises faster. Here are some:

- Know how your organization makes money. Whatever else you do, align your work with some part of that process.
- Document how your contributions support the goals of your organization. Literally show the people around you how you add value. It pays to connect the dots for busy managers who ultimately have to compare you to your coworkers and dole out the raise budget accordingly.

- Be aware of company policy regarding compensation. Some companies are limited by budget constraints, or can only give raises at certain times of the year.
- Have a clear idea of what you want if you ask for a raise. Determine the salary range you're looking for and have a justification for the increase before you make the request.
- Be flexible. How about accepting an extra week of vacation instead of a raise? Or a leave of absence to work for a cause that means a lot to you? Or time to work on a new project you've devised in your own organization?

Whether your organization's philosophy is pay for performance or pay for potential, the considerations we've outlined above all apply: researching salaries and asking for, assessing, and getting what you want. You can find plenty of help online to research compensation and hone your skills. Maximize your baseline salary, and understand that nonmonetary compensation is often as valuable as salary, especially if it involves time off, as we discuss in chapter 5. Most of all, understand that compensation is usually negotiable, and state your case!

CHAPTER 4 **FUSIONS**

- We all work for money, but the importance of money is a matter of degree.
- Understand that all components of pay are negotiable and that you are the chief negotiator.
- An annual 4-percent, pay-for-performance raise works out to about a six-pack of beer per pay period, so try to find a company with a pay-for-potential philosophy.
- There are "cheats" to even the most rigid pay-for-performance plans: for instance, know how your organization makes money and align your work with some part of that process.

CHAPTER 5

What's in It for Me?

"At first, the [Millennials] were the Children of the Rising Dow. They grew up during the greatest period of wealth creation in modern history, but watched their elders consume resources and run up deficits as if the party would never end. Then came the dot-com crash, terrorism, war, climate change. Epic uncertainty informs their worldview."[1]

For Boomers, salary and benefits have been the only road to retirement salvation. Every salary increase, no matter how modest, was something to celebrate. Each extra dollar funded current expenses, compounded over time, and accrued to the all-important retirement account. Increasing salary and incentive pay was the only game around.

As we detailed in chapter 4, for Millennials, salary and benefits are not as important, or—better put—they are not important in the same way. Millennial economic realities are different, as are their perspectives and lifestyles. There is a veritable smorgasbord of incentives and rewards on offer now in most companies, and the philosophy of pay—which had always been based on incremental increases—is changing radically to include not just pay for performance, but pay for potential.

Even though pay may not be a deal-breaker for Millennials initially, earnings potential plays a big role in whether they stay with a company or switch employers. Getting into the minds of Millennials to come up with incentives that truly motivate them, reward them, and keep them from job-hopping is a task that is keeping many thousands of HR and compensation specialists employed.

FUSE TIP

For every ten articles you read on Millennial compensation, five will say salary is key and five will say lifestyle and workplace accommodations are key. Here's the scoop: Millennials expect both.

The best compensation and benefits programs begin by understanding the unique motivational profiles of each employee. That understanding allows flexible compensation programs that recognize specific individual needs and desires. It is especially important to work up these profiles for Millennials, who are accustomed to totally customized interactions in every aspect of their lives.

And yes, we know that setting up customized plans can be a nightmare in big organizations whose HR bureaucracies have outgrown their original purpose of employee service. Our company, FutureSense, is hired all the time to help streamline and innovate compensation and benefits processes. So be of stout heart. It can be done. The key is to have employees manage their salary and benefits package components online, themselves. In other words, make them responsible for meeting enrollment period requirements, filling out forms, reading quarterly reports, etc. Millennials are especially good at this online tasking, and are likely to happily engage in it.

Customized Compensation Plans

Popular thinking on generational differences holds that

- Millennials want fair pay, training opportunities that allow them to grow their careers, and a flexible work schedule.
- Gen-Xers desire work/life balance, immediate money—salary, 401(k) match—and plenty of vacation time.
- Baby Boomers need benefit options for long-term care and want a prestigious-sounding job title and plenty of responsibility.

The crack in this perceptual framework is that it doesn't view the people in these groups as individuals. *In reality, employers have to individually customize compensation plans to attract and retain young employees.* This practice isn't overly tough to do in concept, because it starts out with intuition: You can look at the workforce as a whole and see that older workers want respect and recognition in the form of titles and pay raises. (Given where most of them are in their careers, that's not too surprising.) You can also look at younger workers' lives and see that they want to have more time away from the office, which isn't hard to understand either. They're young, and they want to be out enjoying this time of their lives and doing things that are meaningful to them.

But intuition is not nearly enough. Employers have to do their research. We suggest they simply ask employees what they want, and then provide it—within reason. This is not a revolutionary idea, although it seems to be a revolutionary practice. And it can be difficult to execute, especially with a view to fairness across an entire employee base.

Consider the benefit of paid time off. Most employee surveys show that Boomers rank paid time off far lower than Millennials or Gen-Xers do. Of course they do. Most companies start employees with one week of vacation in the first year, and allot small increases as the years go on. Boomers, who've worked for decades, get four to six weeks of vacation. So Boomers neither need nor desire more paid time off.

So what happens if companies decide to give Millennials—or any employee—the choice of additional time off? There are many ways to do this. The most obvious one is to trade salary increases for time off, or flextime for increased responsibility. The bottom line is that these "soft" incentives can be as valuable as hard cash. And, even if employers are accommodating members of a particular segment within the company, making the accommodation available to everyone and communicating it effectively goes a long way toward both the reality and the perception of fairness.

Online HR materials, especially salary and benefits information, are the way to go. Using online technology capable of communicating the complete cost of employee compensation is a great educational tool that will actually be used. As Art Brooks notes in an article for *Talent Management* magazine, "The cost to maintain [an] employee, including an itemization of salary and all benefits offered, can be an eye-opener for all generations, but especially for those who are younger and may be less familiar with the cost of benefits plans. Online information helps employers sell their organization's offerings." Just as important, employers can solicit feedback on benefit plan offerings through online portals or surveys to determine whether they are meeting employee needs—again, engaging employees by directly asking them what they want.[2]

Companies that use compensation strategies most effectively seem to have two things in common: a willingness to be flexible with all levers of HR practices—including pay, benefits, and other perks—and the ability to make conscious attempts to understand, rather than assume, what drives desired employee engagement.

Especially for Millennials, it's important to tie performance to compensation, shaped by individual employees' priorities. Millennials are merit driven, and they expect to be rewarded for their individual and team efforts.

Again, employers should consider all alternatives to compensating workers for a job well done—not just increasing pay—particularly when another method might be just as effective or even better. Some companies do payroll every week instead of every two weeks to help with cash flow for a generation that likes everything right away. This can also help reduce shrinkage, since an employee who runs out of cash is more likely to skim the register or steal goods. Whatever you decide to do, try something unique. As one HR manager writes: "Benefits are just a list of features; like what you would see on a car. No single element is going to stick out enough unless the benefit is profoundly different from anything else in the marketplace."[3]

A Yahoo! HotJobs/Robert Half International survey shows how Millennial employees across the country ranked company benefits on a scale of 1 (zip) to 10 (most important) in relation to their overall job satisfaction.[4] Not surprisingly, health and dental care, vacation, 401(k), bonuses, and flextime topped the list.

Beyond Base Pay

Especially in the current economic environment of austerity and nascent recovery, and in start-up companies, organizations are trying to find ways to provide compensation "events" that will align their people with organizational success without overburdening their payroll. Translation: We don't pay you more now; we pay you when we win. Then, we can win together. These events or programs include incentives, bonuses, stock options, etc.

The word "incentive" comes from the Latin *incendere*, which means "to kindle or to incite." Organizations use many different types of these programs to motivate and reward especially star or fast-track employees. They range from annual incentives to holiday bonuses, from commissions to gain sharing. Whatever the incentive program offered in your organization, make sure you know how much you might get and for doing what. If you don't know, ask!

A Piece of the Rock

The holy grail of making money has always been stock in the company. If the company grows in value because of the work that you (and your friends) do, you should grow in value, too, right? This is a complicated area, but here is the condensed version of some stock programs:

- Stock options—You are quoted a price now to buy a piece of the rock later; you see how everything goes (does the stock go up or down?) and decide later whether you want to buy at that price.

- Restricted stock—You get a piece of the rock now, but what you can do with it is restricted for a period of time, usually based on your length of employment.
- Phantom stock—You get something that looks, feels, and acts like stock, but you can't vote it (like real owners). However, when the value of the real stock of the company goes up—phantom stock does too!

Body, Mind, and Spirit

When you think you are about to burn out, or if you do actually burn out, does the company have a program for you? Often referred to as benefits plans, these provide health insurance, vacation, and other paid time off, such as leave and holidays. A subset is called employee assistance programs (EAPs). They can include everything from adoption assistance to concierge service (you get your dry cleaning picked up) to day care to grief counseling. Check these plans out—they will give you a pretty good indication of an organization's culture and values. One of the hottest benefits right now is paid time off to work for your favorite charity.

Saving Money for Later

Do you view retirement as so far away that you don't want to think about it now? So did the authors of this book.

Unfortunately, time moves pretty quickly, so socking away money now for use later is a good idea. Your organization probably has something called a 401(k) plan or some other form of deferred compensation. In short, these programs allow you put away money now for use later. Don't get hung up on all the tax consequences—the good news is that if your organization sponsors a plan like this, it usually does so by matching your contributions up to a certain dollar amount. This is free money. Take it. Whether Social Security will be around much longer to help fund anyone's retirement is an open question. So allocate some of your earnings for a 401(k) or an IRA, which can give you a tax deduction and tax-free earnings. You'll be glad you did well before you're retired!

Stroking

In addition to everything mentioned above, what does your organization do to tell you how wonderful you are and to recognize what you have done for them? Do they

- Provide additional time off?
- Recognize you publicly?
- Give you constructive feedback on a regular basis?
- Give you the best postgraduate education (and development opportunities) you could possibly get?

As discussed in earlier chapters, these types of benefits can make a huge difference in how happy you are on the job.

Be aware that there's a danger in forming rigid, static compensation strategies around generations, because individual priorities will change over time. There will always be exceptions. And customized incentives plans are by far the best motivator and retainer.

Which gets back to the main point: Employers should offer a wide range of benefits tailored to the needs of their employees. These potentially include meals and snacks and dry cleaning pick up; family-friendly and flexible work schedules that promote work/life balance; discounts and subsidies such as paying public transportation costs; self-development and educational opportunities; on-site child care; and bonuses and profit sharing.

Accommodate individual desires. It's worth the cost.

CHAPTER 5 **FUSIONS**

- Millennials expect both hard benefits (dollars) and soft benefits (ego and lifestyle boosters).
- Employers should develop a unique motivational profile for each employee, creating a flexible compensation program for all employees.

- The best employers offer a wide range of attractive incentives, from stock options to flextime.
- Everyone needs retirement savings.

CHAPTER 6

Speaking the Language

"Damn! Mad props to her—mad props! I'm so proud of her!"
—seventeen-year-old classmate talking about ninety-eight-year-old Josephine Belasco, who was about to receive her diploma from Galileo High School, eighty years after dropping out.[1]

Why do we need a whole chapter about communication? OMG, aren't we all speaking English? Boomers who have read some of their Millennial coworkers' emails would probably disagree. And Millennials who have sat through too many long meetings or tried to sift through too many endless emails are probably shaking their heads too. The communication differences between generations can be a major source of frustration in the workplace. Think of this chapter as a miniature survival guide to understanding each other and the impact of your own generation's communication habits.

Take a minute to ponder these two quotes:

- "We really want to leverage and monetize our synergy with this new initiative, but there's a disconnect in terms of our reorg."[2]
- "Blogs, Podcasts, Facebook applications, Mobile Apps, Google AdWords, Twitter, Desktop Widgets, FriendFeed, Orkut, RSS. . . . Everyone's talking about it—how to use new media technologies for a corporate or business use. Maybe it's to save money. Or make money. Whatever."[3]

If you're a Digital Native, the first statement will make you LOL (laugh out loud). Or gag. You will totally get the second one.

If you're a Boomer, the reverse will be true.

You are likely not using the same language.

Millennials have their own language, which is verbal, unstructured, abbreviated, and tech-based. It is also global. They think in mosaics, i.e., nonlinear composites of information from disparate sources.

Say what?!

Learning the Language of Millennials

"Since Gutenberg's printing press, the spoken word was a more relaxed version of the structured written word. . . .

This has now changed. For the first time in the English language, we have a growing dichotomy between the written and spoken language. For Millennials, spoken terms are not intended to be written."[4]

We are now employing the first postliterate generation. Boomers are having a hard time with that, embracing a famous *Atlantic* magazine cover that trumpeted: "Is Google Making Us Stoopid?" The working truth is that both generations need to understand the other's style, content, and context of communicating.

Here's how Millennials view communication:

- All information is equal: It all has the same weight regardless of source (Wikipedia is more widely accessed than *Encyclopedia Britannica*).
- An electronic document is more current (and so more accurate) than a printed page.
- Speed is more important than accuracy.
- Visuals are better than text.
- Emoticons (:-)) and novel shorthand spelling ("btw" = "by the way") are the norm in texts, instant messages, and personal emails.
- IM and email are more efficient than face-to-face meetings.
- There is no need to take the time to listen to a voicemail when you see a number on your smartphone—just hit redial.

As one commentator put it, "Gradually, traditional communication methods are being ignored . . . Millennials are entering the workforce and they are wreaking havoc with traditional business communications."[5] Millennials are far from illiterate (even though their grammar and spelling may leave many in doubt); indeed, they are the most educated generation in history. But for employers, the literate forms of communication alone won't connect with Millennials. It is a visual world. Millennials are a multimodal generation, and Boomer bosses need to engage multiple communication channels to get their attention. The more styles you use, the fewer Millennials you'll lose.

FUSE TIP

Balance screen time with face time. Although Millennials may show a preference for electronic communication, have plenty of face-to-face conversations with them. Look them in the eye and test whether you've been heard.

Perfect communications with Millennials start with arresting graphics and limited text; extend through training material that is in game format and employs multimedia Keynote or Prezi rather than PowerPoint; continue through blogs rather than white papers and video rather than text; and end most definitely with short messages rather than long ones. It should come as no surprise that lack of written communications skills is the number one gripe among employers when it comes to Millennials. If Boomer bosses demand that Millennials abide by the rules of grammar, spelling, and scholarship that got Boomers to their leadership roles, they will likely need to provide remedial language arts training, as many companies (and the U.S. Army) have found out. Some organizations also require Millennials to give frequent verbal presentations to wean them off of electronic communication and its hybrid, stylized language.

As communicators, Millennials also tend to tell truth to power: "What's even more frustrating to some . . . managers is Millennials' total disinterest in 'sucking up' and tendency to bluntly tell the manager and other employees exactly what they think of a situation."[6] In other words, they speak what's on their minds. And questions are their communications currency. They will keep probing until they're satisfied that the answers they're getting fit the problem they're trying to solve, a tactic that can appear disingenuous to Boomers.

The Dean of the Haas Business School at the University of California–Berkeley was asked in an interview about candidates for admission calling to ask how to favorably slant their applications. He responded that he viewed the behavior as an opportunity to help develop people who have a different style of communicating into the kinds of leaders that businesses want. "The transparency that allows them to brazenly ask all of those questions is the kind of transparency they have about everything. In regard to government and corporate America, this generation's values are a very good trend. Hopefully it'll have an enormously positive impact."[7]

Millennials speak bluntly, question everything, and are not obsequious. For Boomers who have had years to perfect office politics, these Millennial tendencies can be startling and exasperating. Nor do Millennials care about the protocol for introducing ideas and suggesting change. They'll just lay out what they're thinking.

If you want to learn more about how Millennials communicate (and think), access the same media they do. Read *Wired* magazine, *The Onion*, www.io9.com. Watch *The Daily Show*, *The Colbert Report*, Auto-Tune the News. Get on Ypulse, www.GenerationWhy.com, and www.MillennialsRising.com. Listen to top playlists on Apple's iTunes store, The Hype Machine, and www.BlogTalkRadio.com's Y-Talk radio. Take your time browsing through YouTube videos on any subject matter. Read *HuffPo* or *Perez Hilton* or specialized blogs; there are hundreds on any subject matter. Sign up for a Twitter account and start tweeting.

Most of all, get on Facebook, whose social media technology has changed the world, as described in chapter 11. Millennials see the world, get their news, connect with peers, shop, play games, share their lives, and learn what they need to know through their Facebook pages. Organizations are following their lead, creating identity spaces and inviting customer and client interaction.

As for the new workplace language, there are many excellent and entertaining guides: Mark McCrindle's book, *Word Up*, www.UrbanDictionary.com, and *Newton's Telecom Dictionary* are great. One of our favorite sites is www.BuzzWhack.com, for people who take pleasure in creating a new corporatespeak. Bookmark it. YWIA. (Look it up!)

FUSE TIP

Lighten up the lexicon around your office. Have some fun communicating with employees. Share the latest workplace vocab. It's a great entrée to helping Millennials and Boomers relax and appreciate their differences—and similarities.

From BuzzWhack's homepage, search for "13 Most Fun Buzzwords." Their reader-selected list includes entries like *blamestorming* ("A group process where participants analyze a failed project and look for scapegoats other than themselves"); *clockroaches* ("Employees who spend most of their day watching the clock—instead of doing their jobs"); *plutoed* ("to be unceremoniously dumped or relegated to a lower position without an adequate reason or explanation"); and *muffin top* ("the unsightly roll of flesh that spills over the waist of a pair of too-tight pants"). There is a lot of dark office humor here but also an interesting connection among creative playfulness with words, social trends/fashion/behaviors, and the capacity to invent new products and services.

Learning the Language of Boomers

Speed is important to the younger generation, but by investing a few more minutes communicating with their elder colleagues, Millennials will keep their Boomer coworkers happy (and no one likes to work with grumpy coworkers). Here are a few tips for Millennials hoping to improve communication with their seniors:

- Don't rush meetings and presentations. Build in time for questions and for getting your coworkers' input. Show respect for other opinions. And publicly voice appreciation for any good ideas that come out of the discussion.
- Take an extra minute to review your emails: Are they full of grammatical errors and abbreviations likely to confuse and annoy your Boomer coworkers? Spell-check is amazing. Use it!
- Take a deep breath. Don't let longer Boomer communications frustrate you. Boomers didn't grow up

with texting or Twitter, so keeping notes under 140 characters isn't ingrained in them.

- Include some face-to-face communication. Face-to-face meetings (no, Skype doesn't count) are preferred by older generations, and they build office relationships.
- Be cool. Restrain the urge to rush into a job and change inefficient policies. Understand the thought processes behind the rules. Ask yourself why the policy is in place. Suggest a better one. Understand that changing the rules may crowd some of your Boomer coworkers; they might feel like you're stepping on their toes. Get their input and their consensus.

Finally, don't underestimate your Boomer coworkers: slower communication does not equal slower intelligence. Don't make assumptions about their ability to use today's technology. According to a recent survey by Accenture, "Baby Boomers are embracing popular consumer technology applications nearly twenty times faster than the younger generation."[8]

And whatever you do, bite your tongue before asking them, "Do you know how to use email?" Or, "Are you planning to retire soon?" Or our favorite, "My grandpa gave me that *same* advice!"[9]

Boomers have lingo, too, like *jhobby* ("the act of turning a hobby into a job") and *playcheck* ("Money from a temporary or part-time job taken for the express purpose of funding a trip or other extravagance"). [10]

The Golden Rule

Boomer and Millennial communication has to start from respect.

Millennials can think of Boomer coworkers as a great resource. They have spent at least twice as many years dealing with people and navigating the workplace. Because of this, these coworkers' years of experience make them ideal mentors.

Boomers can realize that the very traits that frustrate them about their Millennial coworkers—namely, their impatience and immediacy—also make them powerful sources of energy, creativity, and idealism. Instead of focusing on what you perceive as younger employees' faults and looking back nostalgically to the way things were in the workplace before they burst onto the scene, imagine their potential and be willing to offer your years of experience as a resource for them. Don't EVER say to them, "You sound *just* like my kid! . . . How old *are* you? Since this is your first job, you probably won't understand. . . ."[11] They may reward you by creating your very own Facebook page!

Communication is enormously important in every organization. Words and how they're used define products and services, report progress and goals, and build relationships with clients and colleagues. Organizations that communicate well internally and externally thrive, especially those that encourage dialogue, questioning, and different communication styles. Those whose communications are blocked have trouble attracting and retaining top employees, finding buyers for their goods, and—quite simply—growing, because they are cutting off the synergies and relationships that come through sharing ideas and perspectives. Recognizing their differences and integrating cogenerational Millennial and Boomer communication styles into organizations is a great way to make sure all voices are heard and all potential customers are welcomed.

CHAPTER 6 **FUSIONS**

- Boomer and Millennial communication has to start with respect.
- Millennials have their own language, which is verbal, unstructured, abbreviated, tech-based, and global.
- Millennials are a multimodal generation, and to connect with them organizations need to communicate in ways that engage multiple learning channels. The more communication styles you use, the fewer Millennials you'll lose.

- If Boomers want to learn more about how Millennials communicate (and think), browse the same media they do.

CHAPTER 7

Becoming the Perfect Plug-and-Play Employee

"The employer generally gets the employees he deserves."
—Sir Walter Gilbey

Google had 3,190,000 results for "perfect employee" when we were getting this chapter ready for publication. That was a lot more manageable than the 24,200,000 it had for "career advice." What employers want seems to be the most thoroughly dissected subject in human history (except, perhaps, finding a soul mate).

Fortunately, much of that wisdom can be neatly distilled into this truism: You want to be the perfect plug-and-play employee, which means the organization that hires you should be able to "plug you in" and you'll start working immediately—just like the hardware on your desktop.

In for-profit organizations, employers are looking for people who will help them make more money than they cost to employ. This is true whether the organization is Boomer or Millennial oriented, whether it employs more creatives or more accountants. For an organization to keep its doors open, it has to bring in enough money to pay the bills. Non-profit employers need people who are externally focused, with demonstrated future-oriented passion for the cause the nonprofit exists to serve.

Skills Employers Want

What does all this mean to the prospective or current employee? Every job has specific requirements regarding education and experience, whether you're entry level or C-level, IT or HR. You either have those requirements or you don't. Specific job requirements aside, there are also broad-based skills that are crucial to your employment at every stage of your career. In interviews, you are likely to be asked hypothetical questions involving dilemmas that feature these skills. Don't despair if you don't yet have them; they can all be learned. Do show that you're aware of how important they are to employers in your answers.

FUSE TIP

On size doesn't fit all. Be sure the personal values of employees mash up, not match up, with company values when you hire for fit. Compatibility and job success require skills and mind-sets that are complementary—not identical—to your company and its brand image.

Here is our annotated list of the top ten skills most sought after by employers:

Communications

This is by far the most desired skill. It involves communicating clearly, both verbally and in writing, inside the organization and out, with managers and customers alike.

Interpersonal Skills

Having relationships with colleagues and customers, collaborating with others, and resolving conflicts with coworkers are all crucial workplace skills.

Analytical Skills

The ability to analyze is not limited just to spreadsheets. This is problem solving through identifying issues; assessing situations; synthesizing peer, manager, and customer perspectives; and obtaining relevant additional information.

Technological Literacy

Technological literacy goes way beyond baseline proficiency. The skill of making memorable visual presentations takes more than *inputting* words on slides; it begs for skill in *choreographing* MP3 files, video, Flash, hyperlinks, and interactive graphics to communicate with widely disparate audiences. So, too, the skill of entering numbers into a spreadsheet is *manipulating* data. The true need is for *managing* data—getting the best input available in global databases and developing "what if" scenarios to solve your organization's issues and move it forward. In other words, saying you know how to use a software application goes way beyond booting it up; you need to understand what the application can do and to use it to its full advantage.

Flexibility and Resiliency

Job descriptions are not set in concrete, and goals are rarely achieved in a straight-line fashion. Employees have to be flexible in their outlook and approach to their work. This includes multitasking; setting priorities; adapting to changing conditions, work assignments, and new team members; accepting new ideas and instructions; and, figuring out how to reach goals even as they are constantly evolving. Resilience is a huge skill; always having a Plan B when your original way forward is blocked will ensure career longevity. We guarantee that you will be asked in job interviews how you overcome obstacles and how you react when things don't go your way. Be prepared!

Leadership and Management Skills

Cowboys do not make good employees. Organizations are teams that need to be led, with projects that need to be managed. Career advancement is based on presenting your viewpoint and getting others to follow your lead. Stars are made by taking responsibility for a project and managing coworkers to meet goals.

Respect for Others

True respect for diverse colleagues and customers involves showing both a sensitivity to and an awareness of other people's differences and cultures, and sharing your own culture and viewpoint. It's not enough to treat everyone the same.

Time Management

What worked in college—"I always work best under pressure"—as deadlines loomed is not what employers want to see. Managing your time means spacing your work in increments and keeping your boss informed that you are on target.

Creative Problem Solving

This was known in twentieth-century workplaces as "thinking outside the box." There is no box anymore in our twenty-first-century offices. Employers expect you to bring life experience and full Internet proficiency to problem solving, meeting goals using creativity, reason, collaboration, and real-time resources.

Values Employers Want

Beyond these top skills, employers also want whole people. Equally important to hard and soft skills are the values and character traits that consistently appear on twenty-first-century employer must-have lists. Google advertises directly to prospective employees who have the attitude and values they want: “Into being challenged? Into having fun? Want to change the world? If the answer is yes, then you’ve come to the right place. . . . [Google] continues to look for those who share an obsessive commitment to creating search perfection and having a great time doing it.”[1]

Here are the top ten personal attributes employers want prospective employees to demonstrate:

Self-Confidence

If you don’t believe in yourself, in your unique mix of skills, education, and abilities, why should a prospective employer? Be confident in yourself and what you can offer employers.

Self-Management

This means getting things done on time without wasting time or resources—yours or the organization’s. It involves scheduling your time, marshaling your resources, and maintaining your energy. It means minimizing interruptions and time-wasters, doing what you say you’re going to do—on schedule and without supervision.

Personal Accountability

Personal accountability means owning your performance at work, and not blaming others when things go wrong. If you make a mistake, own it, accept responsibility for it, and learn from it. Take responsibility for getting along with others, as a leader and as a member of a team.

Results Orientation

This is the ability to meet schedules, deadlines, and performance goals. It is also known as keeping your eye on the ball. Results always matter, process less so.

Integrity and Honesty

Employers probably respect personal integrity more than any other value, especially in light of recent corporate scandals. Don't compromise yours by small acts of dishonesty, such as pilfering from the supply cabinet, copying software programs for your own use, or fibbing to save face. The perception of your integrity is the building block of your relationships and the key to your advancement. It is almost impossible to repair once it is damaged.

Dedication, and Work Ethic

Employers want workers who love what they do and will keep at it until they get the job done. This begins with arriving at work every day on time and ready to work. It means being reliable as a teammate. It means getting the job done, no matter what it takes. You may choose not to buy into this expectation, but be aware that your performance along these lines will be viewed as a measure of your commitment to your job and to the organization.

Loyalty

Employers want workers with a strong devotion to the organization. This means someone who will place its goals above her own personal interests, even if the organization is not always loyal in return. Again, you may choose not to play, but you will be scored on this.

Positive Attitude, Energy, and Passion

Applicants who get hired and employees who get promoted are the ones with zeal. They show drive and high energy through both words and actions. Most of all, employers love to see passion for their products and services, because they know that employees with that emotional commitment will be their best workers, ambassadors, and salespeople.

Professionalism

This means acting responsibly and fairly in all your personal and work activities, which is seen as a sign of maturity and self-confidence. It means dressing for the part; no sandals or muffin tops in the office. Gossip, pettiness, and vindictiveness are never valued. Office language is business-speak, not hipster.

Willingness to Learn

You should always be willing to learn new skills. Jobs are constantly changing and evolving, and you need to grow in sync.

In addition to this list of top character traits, we have found several other qualities to be useful in our own training and consulting work:

- Openness to sharing ideas
- Ability to work under pressure
- Willingness to take strategic risks without unwarranted fear
- Understanding of business strategy and how the company creates stakeholder (shareholder, customer, employee, and community) value

There are no perfect hires or perfect employees. Everyone is brought on board and promoted based on a calculated risk of whether they can do the specific job on offer, grow to take on additional jobs in the organization, and fit well into the organization. The skills and character traits we've listed are universally sought; how they're put together is the unique package that each prospective and current employee has to offer. Many of the skills are learned through experience;

many of the character traits are developed over time. Being aware of their value to employers and then demonstrating your mastery makes you into the perfect plug-and-play employee.

CHAPTER 7 **FUSIONS**

- For-profit organizations are looking for people who will help make them more money than they will cost the organization.
- For nonprofits, employers need people with externally focused, future-oriented passion for the cause the nonprofit serves.
- There are broad-based skills that are crucial to your employment at every stage of your career, starting with communications and interpersonal abilities.
- There are also character traits/values that are crucial to your employment at every stage of your career, including self-confidence, integrity, and work ethic.
- Certain skills and character traits are universally sought; how they're put together is the unique package that each prospective and current employee has to offer.

CHAPTER 8

Eighty Percent of Success Is Showing Up & Other Career Myths Busted

"It's not who you are underneath; it's what you do that defines you."
—Batman Begins, *2005*

Filmmaker Woody Allen is credited with saying that 80 percent of success is showing up. Apple CEO Steve Jobs said that it's better to be a pirate than to join the navy. And business writer Hal Lancaster has suggested that getting fired is nature's way of telling you that you had the wrong job in the first place.

What do these sayings have in common (besides some humor)?

A grain of truth and a lot of myth. This chapter takes a playful but discerning look at common workplace myths that can hamper both Millennials' and Boomers' peace, productivity, promotion, and prosperity.

The Top 12 Workplace Myths, as Commonly Misunderstood by All Generations

We've put this idiosyncratic list together over the many years we've been in the consulting business. These myths seem to cause most workplace misunderstandings and career catastrophes. They are pretty much in order of how frequently we experience their fallout in our work, from least to most (in reverse order, to save the denouement for the end!).

12. You have to like your job to be happy.

Partially true. You spend three-fourths of your waking hours at work, so enjoying that time is pretty important. But the correlation between your happiness and your job can be overrated. The most important factors for happiness are strong personal relationships and meaningful life activities. If you have great friends, family, and outside interests, you can probably be happy even if you hate your job. (Imagine a Porta-Potty cleaner who's in love, or someone in a so-so job who spends his free time volunteering at a community food bank.) According to a 2010 study conducted by The Conference Board, Americans are increasingly unhappy with their jobs: only 45 percent claim to be satisfied, and roughly 64 percent of workers under twenty-five say they are unhappy in their jobs. That said, if you truly hate your job and it's making you miserable, you should leave it.

FUSE TIP

Don't let people who hate their jobs poison the well in your organization. Move them over or out as fast as you can, without hesitation. They'll thank you for it, some day, and so will everyone else pretty quickly.

11. The glass ceiling doesn't exist anymore.

Yes it does. The Millennials who reviewed the draft of this book had never heard of the glass ceiling. They had yet to encounter one, except perhaps at a hot dance club, so they were intrigued to learn that it is a barrier to upward mobility formed by the prejudice of those in charge against those who are not like them. The phrase "glass ceiling" is usually shorthand for male bosses keeping female workers in lower-paying, nonexecutive jobs when the women can see better jobs above them. News flash: Women still do not have the same opportunities for advancement as men. The Fortune 500 CEO list contains fifteen females. The boards of directors of the Inc. 1000 include only a handful of females. The recession has caused the earnings gap between men and women to shrink, but according to *USA Today*, women still earn only 82.8 percent of the median weekly wage of men.[1] You do the math. While you're at it, try to find executives of major firms who are people of color, gay or lesbian, disabled, etc. They are rarer than hen's teeth. Millennials can change this, joining those Boomers who have worked to change it for years.

10. The hardest workers get promoted.

Nope. The most likable people get promoted. Your mother was right: Good social skills are crucial to your career. Across the board, people would rather work with someone who is likable and incompetent than with someone who is skilled and obnoxious. As Tiziana Casciaro of Harvard Business School says, "How we value competence changes depending on whether we like someone or not." Besides, people lacking social grace are perceived to lack other life and work competencies as well. If you are currently invested in this myth, *Emotional Intelligence* by Daniel Goleman (Bantam, 2005) is a good guide. It will tell you what you need to know to build and accurately assess relationships. Our advice is to open yourself up to possibilities and explore the greatest potential of your unique personality, learning what you need to do to become more likable.

9. Everyone has sex with coworkers.

Sorry, no. Everyone might *think* about having sex with someone in the office, but many people allow their forward brains to take precedence in the office setting. However, many of us can chalk up an office romance or two. And why not? The workplace offers opportunity (men and women together), motive (anti-boredom), and geographic convenience (most employees live within a reasonable distance of the office). In fact, 41 percent of employed Americans aged twenty-five to forty have admitted to having engaged in an office romance, according to a joint survey sponsored by *Glamour* magazine and www.Lawyers.com.[2] Here's the kicker: Employers had the most problems with office dalliances when the romance involved a manager dating a reporting staff person. And remember, the specter of sexual harassment is always present—especially once the affair is over. Most important, keep sexting out of the work environment. It is universally banned, for good reason.

8. Office politics is about backstabbing.

Wrong again. Sure, some long knives will be out wherever you go, but office politics can also be about helping people get what they want. Figuring out what coworkers care about, and how to help them get it, obviates the need to strong-arm, disparage, or manipulate them. We don't mean to say that you can bare your soul to colleagues and expect your confidences to be kept anymore than you would expect that in a random group of acquaintances. Jealousy will still rear its ugly head. Use your judgment. Become politically savvy!

FUSE TIP

Share the *Idiot's Guide to Office Politics* or your personal battle stories with young employees. Millennials may need a crash course. Make this part of a mentoring or orientation process so they get off on the right foot.

7. Do good work and you'll do fine.

Nope. As writer Sam Ewing says, "It's not the hours you put in your work that counts, it's the work you put in the hours." And no one will *know* what you're doing in your cube unless you *tell* them. Let people know what you're working on and tell them—especially your manager and manager's manager—about its success. No one else will do it for you. Recognize that self-promotion is an art form; be careful that you don't oversell. Don't take credit for someone else's good work. Give your colleagues the credit they deserve and you will stand out.

6. A great résumé will get you hired.

Not true. Only 10 percent of jobs come from sending

unsolicited résumés. Most jobs come from people leveraging their networks. When you make a connection with a prospective employer, your résumé will simply be glanced at to make sure you have the required skills and to check for obvious problems. Expand your network instead of obsessing over which descriptive adjective best describes your PowerPoint skills. And *never* lie or experiment with the truth on your résumé. You will be found out and fired. And don't forget that employers today are checking Facebook pages faster than other references. Make sure yours doesn't show a side of you that makes you an undesirable hire.

5. It's better to emulate Donald Trump than to be yourself.

Nope. It's better to *be yourself* and to keep learning. As Penelope Trunk writes on Guy Kawasaki's blog, "Figure out how to do what you love, follow your heart's desire, and you'll be great at it. Those who stand out as leaders have a notable authenticity that enables them to make genuinely meaningful connections with a wide range of people."[3]

4. Millennials don't work for the money but for the fulfillment.

Nonsense. Ask yourself again: If you won the lottery tomorrow, would you go back to your job the next day? Work is about money—see the previous chapters on this topic. Money is about freedom to make life choices.

3. Email is always the most efficient communication method.

No! It's hard to remember how we got along without email, but it's decidedly misused and over-relied upon today. Calling a person or having face time with him can minimize confusion, and builds relationships. Without visual and auditory cues, people often misinterpret the intent and message of emails, even if you use those perky emoticons :-) (which is why they were invented). Face-to-face rules; voice is good; email is third choice.[4]

FUSE TIP

Sleep isn't overrated. Insomniacs need to resist the temptation to reply to email in the wee hours or they risk creating a workforce that never sleeps.

2. The generation gap between Boomer bosses and Millennial workers hampers productivity and the pursuit of workplace happiness.

Maybe yes, maybe no. Although there is clearly an age difference, we argue strongly that it's not a gap but a mash-up, a potential fusion and cogenerational melding that leverages skills, attributes, and perspectives. If we focus on the gap, we impede the possibilities. Clearly people of different age groups see the world in different ways and bring different experience and skills to the table. Lassoing those skills to get that bronco moving forward with all of its energy intact is the goal. It's like any other relationship issue: If you ignore it, the relationship will fail. As research scientist Jennifer Deal notes, "The so-called generation gap is, in large part, the result of miscommunication and misunderstanding, fueled by common insecurities and the desire for clout."[5]

1. You can have it all.

Absolutely not. This is the biggest myth of all. Here's how it works in real life: You can have the things you want most only intermittently. That means sometimes your job comes first. Sometimes your family. Sometimes you. Your priorities will never line up like bars on a slot machine. Chasing this dream will ruin you. But the clearer you are about your priorities and setting boundaries, the better your chances of striking your personal balance. At least on some days! This truth about not having it all is universal, not generational.

As the philosopher and psychologist William James said, "Happiness is reflected in the ratio of one's accomplishments to one's aspirations. This suggests, of course, that when it comes to feeling happy in our lives, we can choose one of two paths: continually add to our list of accomplishments—or lower our expectations." We would add a third path: a career path free of illusion. Myths are by definition illusions, widely held cultural beliefs that live at the intersection of imagination and reality. They often inspire us to greater efforts. An uncritical belief in them, however, skews our understanding of reality. Better to be myth-busters than misanthropes.

CHAPTER 8 **FUSIONS**

- The most likable people get promoted, not the hardest workers.
- Broadcast the work you're doing, especially to your managers.
- Be yourself. Really.
- Without visual and auditory cues, people often misinterpret an email's intent and message.
- You cannot have it all. You can have the things you want most only intermittently.

CHAPTER 9

They Can't Do That, Can They?

"From the employer's point of view, if you haven't mastered the simple art of presenting yourself appropriately, you probably haven't mastered the more important, complicated skills required in the workplace."[1]

The workplace is not a democracy. It has rules and regulations that you must abide by or you'll pass Go without collecting $200. That's as true for Millennials entering the workforce as for Boomers who are still there or trying to reenter it.

Most of these rules combine pomposity with legalese, which makes for a deadly combination. Nonetheless, there is usually a seed of something you need to know buried in the verbiage. Uncover it or it'll eat you alive, just like

Audrey II relished her unsuspecting victims in *Little Shop of Horrors*.

Employment law keeps many thousands of lawyers employed. These laws are a morass of federal, state, and local regulation. You have to know enough to keep your job and protect your rights. Most of what you need to know is in your trusty code of corporate conduct, aka your employee handbook. This tome can run to more than a hundred single-spaced pages in a big company. On your first day of work, you'll have to sign a form declaring that you've read and understood this puppy.

FUSE TIP

Rule breakers don't read the rule book. Simply expecting a Millennial to read a book of policies is a mistake. Cover the highlights in a face-to-face orientation if you want Millennials to understand what it means to play by the rules.

Some companies have uploaded their entire handbook online. Do they really think that makes it easier to digest? The most Millennial-friendly companies, such as Sun Microsystems, have created interactive online game content that explains corporate rules. You can create an avatar and role-play various corporate scenarios. However the corporate holy book is presented in your on-boarding process, pay attention. To play the game you have to at least skim the table of contents and zero in on the essentials.

Keep to the Code

Here are the cheats—the parts of the code you've absolutely got to get and abide by.

At-Will Employment

This is the right of employers to fire employees for any reason, or for no reason at all, at any time. It also gives employees the legal right to quit their jobs at any time for any reason. Even so, employers may not fire employees in a way that discriminates, violates public policy, or conflicts with written or implied promises they make concerning the length of employment or grounds for termination. Almost all employees are at-will employees.

Translation: If your employer decides to let you go, that's the end of your job—and you have very limited legal rights to fight it.

Equal Employment Opportunity

Equal employment opportunity (EEO) laws require that all employment decisions—hiring, promotion, transfer, compensation, benefits, discipline, termination—have to be made without regard to race, color, religion, sex, sexual orientation, gender identity, age, disability, national origin, citizenship/immigration status, veteran status, or any other protected status.

Translation: No one can be discriminated against in the workplace, compliments of federal law.

Sexual and Other Unlawful Harassment

Pay attention to these laws and regulations, as they are very different from current American culture, especially the hook-up world of Millennials. Unwelcome sexual advances, requests for sexual favors, and other verbal or physical conduct of a sexual nature constitute sexual harassment when submitting to or rejecting it may affect someone's employment, unreasonably interfere with someone's work performance, or create an intimidating, hostile, or offensive work environment. This includes sexting.

Translation: If your mother would yell at you for the behavior, or if you think it even *might* be offensive, it probably is. Don't do it on the job, especially if testosterone or estrogen is clouding your thinking.

For a great article on some of the most notorious harassment cases ever, go to www.HRWorld.com and search for "The Top 20 Sexual-Harassment Cases of All Time."

FUSE TIP

Millennials have redefined relationships. Boundaries differ for "friends with benefits" situations. In the workplace, casual sex between friends may cloud perceptions of harassment. Making sure Millennials understand the organization's rules on sex in the workplace, and what constitutes harassment, could save large legal fines later on.

Standards of Conduct

This is a list of guidelines regarding ethical and legal standards all employees are expected to follow on the job; if you don't, you can be disciplined or fired. Take Mark Hurd, the former CEO of Hewlett-Packard, who was dismissed for making inappropriate use of corporate funds when he paid a woman with whom he had an admittedly nonsexual relationship to make HP product videos. Standards can also apply even when you're not at work but are engaging in illegal or morally questionable acts. For example, employers do not find drug use, drunkenness, or public sex acceptable—on or off the job.

Translation: You are what you do. And when you're in public, all behavior is public. Picture your boss watching you drunkenly hurl on YouTube. Not a pretty sight.

Workplace Searches

This is language typically found in employee handbooks: "To protect the property and ensure the safety of all employees . . . the company reserves the right to conduct personal searches consistent with state law . . . and to inspect any possessions carried to and from the company's property . . . Because searches may result in the discovery of personal possessions or documents, employees should refrain from bringing to or creating in the workplace any item or personal property they do not wish to reveal. . . ."

Translation: Your personal and work property can be searched at any time, for no reason. Don't bring contraband to work, and don't create unauthorized material while you're in the office.

Personnel Files

Remember in junior high when you heard during every trip to the principal's office, "That will go on your permanent record"? Workplaces have permanent records too. They're called personnel files. They typically include your employment application, job references, results from any employment aptitude testing, school transcripts or degree verifications, performance reports, a documented disciplinary action history, a résumé, a signed employee handbook form, at-will employment sign-off sheets, current personal information, and a family emergency contact form. In most states, employees can view their files, with a supervisor present, when they ask in writing. For privacy reasons, your payroll information and medical information are not included in this file. For the same reason, prospective employers cannot see or be told any information in your file, including performance reviews. To get around this stricture, many organizations are now asking prospective employees to bring a copy of their latest performance review to job interviews.

Translation: Everything you do in the workplace goes in a paper file and will follow you throughout your employment at each organization.

Exempt vs. Nonexempt Status

It's important to know whether your job is classified as exempt or nonexempt. Nonexempt employees are entitled to overtime pay. Exempt employees are not. These exemptions are determined by very complicated federal regulations regarding your pay and your job duties. Job titles do not determine exempt or nonexempt status.[2]

Translation: Ask Human Resources whether your job is exempt or nonexempt. If the government says you should be paid overtime, you need to get paid overtime.

Pay Periods

State and federal laws regulate the timing of when you get paid. Most states require wages for most types of workers to be paid at least twice during each calendar month on days designated in advance as regular paydays, although some employees get paid only once a month. Employers have to post a notice with this information. Overtime wages must be paid in the payroll period following the period they were earned. If you're fired, all wages, including accrued vacation, must be paid immediately at the time you're let go.

Translation: How and when you get paid is regulated by law, not the whim of your employer. Most employees will get paid twice a month on a regular basis. Ask your HR person. This is handy to know, especially for Millennials who may be paying rent and bills for the first time.

Hours of Work

We've already covered the point that employers expect workers to show up on time and ready to work. Scheduling is controlled by the organization; total hours of work are defined by law. Employers know that many workers tend to slack off during the day; according to a 2005 survey by America Online and www.Salary.com, the average worker admits to wasting 2.09 hours per eight-hour workday, not including lunch and permitted breaks.[3] To combat this as best they can, most employers set up a specific policy on work hours.

Here's typical language used in an employee handbook section on work hours:

> Company work hours are _____ a.m. to ______ p.m. Monday through Friday, with one (unpaid) hour for lunch. Nonexempt employees receive two ten-minute paid break periods for each full workday, one at mid-morning and one at mid-afternoon, and are expected to take a lunch or meal break midway through their shift. As for overtime, all nonexempt employees who work more than eight hours in one workday will receive overtime pay at the rate of one and a half times the employee's regular rate of pay for all hours worked in excess of eight hours in one workday or forty hours in one workweek, or in any higher amounts required by law.

Translation: Know what's expected in terms of daily hours. If you're told to be at work at 8:45 a.m. and to leave at 5:15 p.m. and you can't negotiate flextime, be there preferably before 8:45 and don't leave until at least 5:15. Start and end times are not movable feasts without buy-in from your manager, no matter how unnecessary they may appear. Also know the larger work time issues—vacation, holidays, sick leave, etc. These are benefits to be earned or negotiated, and they can be worth more to you than salary, as we explain in chapters 3 through 5.

For more information on federal laws on work hours, check out the subtopics under the "Work Hours" page on the U.S. Department of Labor's website.[4]

Performance Reviews

Remember feeling queasy when report cards came out? You still can! At most companies, workers get annual employee performance reviews, where your job performance is evaluated by your manager or boss. Reviews often determine raises, bonuses, promotions, new opportunities, and sometimes whether you keep your job.

Just like in school, meeting your job requirements just means you're adequate—nothing more. To get a better review and the goodies that go with it, figure out how to do more to enhance your overall performance and your organization's goals. Make sure your manager knows your work product, and keep a portfolio of it yourself, along with any positive comments from colleagues, clients, or customers.

Translation: You're still getting graded. But now grades mean more money, bigger bonuses, better benefits (such as more vacation and stock options), and better assignments. It is up to you to manage your performance and review—show your work to your advantage and do not be passive. Ask for more frequent reviews.

FUSE TIP

Instant performance feedback is gratifying. Millennials hate surprises when it comes to performance problems. Remember this from chapter 1: Don't delay when giving feedback. Give younger employees a chance to learn from their mistakes or revel in their accomplishments in real time.

Workplace Dress Code and Grooming

What you look like matters, no matter where you work. www.TheSmokingGun.com posted the Hooters employee handbook on its site, which contained this classic line: "Only approved Orange Hooters Girl Shorts are to be worn, sized to fit, and should NOT BE SO TIGHT THAT THE BUTTOCKS SHOW." Employers can limit employees' personal expression on the job—as in clothing, grooming, and body art choices—so long as they do not impinge on your civil liberties. Your employer will have a dress and grooming code in the handbook. They can mandate uniforms, hair length, jewelry, and more. Some of this may be for safety's sake, but most is in aid of running a business that attracts paying clients.

We suggest being clean, not wearing perfume, and understanding that different regions have different dress codes.

Men still wear suits to the office in Chicago, but they rarely do anywhere in California. The advice from *Glamour*'s fashion editor and other fashion mavens is basic: dress for the job you want, not the one you have; dress the way your boss does; and wear clothes that look good on you. Dress codes routinely ban tank tops, halter tops, muscle shirts, clothing with foul language or obscene images on it, torn clothing, sweatpants and sweat suits, flip-flops, and hats, among other items. Lack of proper undergarments is taboo. So is visible cleavage—unless you're working at Hooters!

Be aware that jobs involving face-to-face client contact will almost always require a more professional look, no matter how casual Fridays are. Also note that prejudice still exists within corporate America about tattoos and piercings. So cover up the tats or pay the consequences.

For a guide to appropriate dress, see Donald K. Burleson's hilarious illustrated guide to professional dress code.[5] A more serious take on dress and etiquette for men is Clint Greenleaf's *The Unwritten Rules of the Workplace.*[6]

Translation: Like it or not, we are all immediately judged by our appearance. Employers can dictate your clothing and grooming.

Telephone, Email, Texting, and Facebook

Keep personal use of phones and email, and all use of texting and social media, to a minimum in the workplace. Generally speaking, if your employer gives you notice—in the handbook, for example—that you have no reasonable expectation of privacy, you don't. Your phone calls, emails, and any voice mail messages can be monitored and are usually archived. We can't overstress this—*do not say or write anything in the workplace setting that can come back to bite you*. Because it will.

Another important point is that *how* you say things, especially electronically, is as important as *what* you say. Humans are visual thinkers and learners. Human brains are built to decode visual cues as they take in left-brain information. Absent these visual cues, the receiver's personality will supply the emotional context—and it may not be a good context if the recipient is paranoid or aggressive. Reread your emails and consider your specific recipient before you hit Send. Think about your tone of voice during phone calls and when leaving voice mail messages. If you wouldn't want to receive the message, don't send it. Face-to-face communication is almost always best whenever it's possible.

Translation: You have no right to private communication in the workplace. Practice restraint in your communications, especially emails.

Postage, Shipping, Copying, and Office Supplies

They are *not* yours for personal use, even if there's a warehouse full of supplies, a room full of high-end color copiers, an unsecured postage meter, and an open account for FedEx. These are corporate assets. They fall under somebody's budget and audit. If you take or partake without authorization, it's stealing. You will be disciplined or fired, and your entire character will come into question. Why risk it for a few bucks of free stuff?

Translation: Buy your own office supplies and stamps for your personal use.

Employment Benefits

Benefits eligibility, medical insurance, 401(k) match, stock options, employee discounts, tuition reimbursement, and workers' compensation are all important to you because they equate to money in your pocket now and in the future. And, as we've said before, some benefits are worth more than salary and raises because they give you a hook into the future, more time, peace of mind, etc.

Translation: Snuggle up with the employee benefits information and get to know your total compensation package.

Immigration Status

Federal law requires that all employers complete and retain an Employment Eligibility Verification Form (I-9) for each person they hire for employment in the United States. This includes citizens and noncitizens.

Translation: There's no getting around this requirement. Employers face big fines if they do not comply.

Computer Software Licensing

Unauthorized duplication of computer software is a federal

offense, punishable by up to a $250,000 fine and up to five years in jail. Enterprise software and shareware is anathema to organizations, as it can corrupt authorized software and foul up networks, platforms, and servers, to say nothing of reducing bandwidth to a squeak and hammering holes in security protocols and firewalls.

Translation: Don't illegally duplicate software. Don't download *any* software or products without approval from your IT department.

Privacy

Hiring is serious business. Quite literally, each hire can be a million-dollar decision if you look at average employee costs over an average career span.

Privacy Is an Illusion.
Employers Do Background Checks

To hedge their bets and tilt the odds in favor of an excellent hiring decision, employers have a variety of selection tools at their disposal, starting with stated qualifications—such as GPA and technical proficiency—extending to interview questions designed to trap the unwary and throw them back into the unemployment pool, and culminating in a thorough look into your public records and recorded private life. Especially since 9/11, background checks themselves have become a billion-dollar business.

So be aware that prospective employers very likely will

do a background check on you. Background reports can range from a verification of an applicant's Social Security number to a detailed account of a potential employee's history and acquaintances. Many employers are now searching MySpace and Facebook for the profiles of applicants. And note that almost as many employers search such sites for information about current employees.

Here are some of the pieces of information that might be included in a background check according to www.PrivacyRights.org.[7] Many are public records created by government agencies.

- Driving records
- Vehicle registration
- Credit records
- Criminal records
- Social Security number
- Education records
- Court records
- Workers' compensation
- Bankruptcy
- Character references
- Neighbor interviews
- Medical records
- Property ownership
- Military records
- State licensing records
- Drug test records
- Past employers
- Personal references
- Incarceration records
- Sex offender lists

Be acutely aware that in the age of media 2.0, *there is no privacy*. Act and record accordingly. If you have subpar credit, have been convicted of a crime, or have failed a drug test, be prepared to discuss the circumstances and lessons learned if the subject is brought up. Vet your profiles on social networking sites. If you have pictures or random thoughts or even links that would embarrass your mother, they can kill your chances with a prospective employer.

If you want to know more workplace rules and regulations, ask your HR manager. If you want to know more than that, check out these sites:

- The U.S. Equal Employment Opportunity Commission (www.EEOC.gov) is a federal government agency that protects and advocates for employees' rights.
- The National Labor Relations Board (www.NLRB.gov) gives information on labor union and workplace rights.
- www.Nolo.com is an amazing organization that prints law books. Its employee-rights resource center is an excellent repository of information.
- www.Employment.FindLaw.com has an employee-rights center that provides helpful information on the legal rights of workers in all phases of employment.

The answer to the question posed by the chapter title, "They Can't Do That, Can They?" is yes, they certainly can. These are workplace codes and rules to be bucked at your own peril, and ignoring them may embroil you and/

or the organization that employs you in a lawsuit. They are not the places to proclaim your individuality or Ayn Rand sense of self. Boomers can be great workplace guides for Millennials in word and in deed, helping newbies understand the world of work and avoid pitfalls, pratfalls, and scenes from *The Office*.

CHAPTER 9 **FUSIONS**

- The workplace is not a democracy.
- At least skim the table of contents and zero in on the essentials of your company's employee handbook.
- Almost all employees are at-will employees, who can be fired for any reason or for no reason at all, at any time (within public policy constraints). Employees have the legal right to quit their jobs at any time, for any reason, too.
- Know what sexual harassment is and what to do about it.
- You are what you do. All behavior is public.
- Your appearance matters, especially if you're working with customers in person.
- You have no right to privacy in the workplace.

CHAPTER 10

Is Your 9 to 5 the Night of the Living Dead?

"Believe in yourself."
—The Wizard of Oz to Dorothy

Now you know what employers want, and you've landed that perfect job. Why, then, do you suddenly feel like you want to throw up every morning before going to work? Do you recognize yourself in this scenario?

> Sales meetings bear a cult's telltale signs: leader (an over-caffeinated VP of sales), mantra ('Accelerate in 2008!'), big production number ('The Future's So Bright, I Gotta Wear Shades'), and ritualistic insignia (logo-emblazoned totes). I sit in the back where nobody can catch me scrawling 'KILL ME PLEASE' on my handout.[1]

Most likely you don't need a Clearblue Easy Digital Pregnancy Test to help figure out that nausea you experience each morning on the way to work, but you may well need some soul-searching, psyche-plumbing dialogue with yourself to figure out the gap between the job you thought you got and the one you really have.

In other words, stellar expectations about their jobs is a classic trait among Millennials, yet *The Office* is one of their favorite shows. Reality is somewhere between the two.

And for Boomers, you are still trying to write (yet again) the survival guide to your job, even though many of you thought you would be done by now. Think about it this way: We liked Ted Danson in *Cheers* (when he had dark hair). Now he has shockingly white hair in *Bored to Death*.

What do you do with this feeling of dread? Pay attention if you have any of the following symptoms (or you notice another employee or colleague who does):[2]

You feel sick. Being unhappy at work can damage your health. If you're not clubbing every night, then the nausea, migraines, backaches, impotence, and insomnia you might be experiencing are signs of excess stress. Your mental health can also be damaged, along with your personal relationships.

You're out of the loop. Some of your projects have been reassigned; you're left out of important meetings or email strings. Ask your boss for the 411, but understand that this treatment is most often a way of asking you to leave.

Personnel changes impact you. Your favorite boss moves on, or moves you out. You no longer have access to power, plum projects, or the decision-making process. These changes may start small, but the cumulative effect on your status can be large.

Your expertise becomes part of the background scenery. Your great work makes you the new "plug-and-play"—the expert in your area. You're pigeonholed, or you become known as the good corporate citizen who'll do whatever you're asked (that no one else will put up with)—flying red-eyes to meet clients, relocating to strange cities, working 24/7 while others get to have real lives.

FUSE TIP

Don't bleed Boomers. They have their hands full these days with boomerang kids and frail parents. Show them some love, too, or you risk being robbed of vital institutional memory and perspective.

You outgrow your job. You have *über* experience to do your job but not the confidence to move elsewhere.

You're praying for a better offer. You've had the same salary for too long, with no increase in sight. Even jobs in Detroit look good.

Work is interfering with what's important in your life. Are you balancing job and family and health and relationships and social causes? Are you renewing yourself with nonwork activities? Are you motivated by what Jim Collins calls big, hairy, audacious goals? Too much work makes you dull . . . and resentful.

Boredom. Boredom is a killer. It makes you scattered, mildly depressed, and take forever to do simple tasks. You spend way too much time on Facebook and Farmville. You need challenges and opportunities to reawaken the slumbering Horatio Alger.

You're angry but can't figure out why. Anger makes you cranky, and no matter how great your work is, if you become a depressing crank, colleagues will avoid you. This isolation limits your mobility and can make you a target in a layoff or reorganization.

FUSE TIP

Nip anger in the bud, or else. Angry people, no matter how old, will sour the workplace. Establish a zero-tolerance approach, especially if anger is taken out on colleagues from a different generation.

Your organization is going downhill. If your employer is losing customers, losing money, and losing employees, look out for number one—you.

FUSE TIP

Millennials are not afraid to jump ship into shark-infested waters. Getting out is easy for Millennials despite a bad economy. Woo those who are key to your success with a mix of sweet incentives and development opportunities.

Your relationship with your boss is damaged beyond repair. You've tried to fix it, but it's hopeless. If it's your fault—you've played hooky, blown deadlines, etc.—move on and don't repeat your miscreant behavior in your next job. If your boss is at fault, read *The No A**hole Rule* by Robert I. Sutton.[3]

Your life has changed. Perhaps you've married (remarried) or started a (second) family and the salary and benefits no longer support you. You have to accurately assess what you need to do for your family.

Your values are not in sync with the work culture. Does your company have a dress code and you shop at

Goodwill? Or do people who treat others disrespectfully still get promoted? Or are staff instructed to leave every light blazing at night to deter burglars, and you want to go minimize your carbon footprint? Whatever the clash of values, divergence will damage your happiness at work.

Your company is ethically challenged. Managers lie to customers about product quality and want you to equivocate about the day products will ship. The company is stealing information from competitors, or they are cooking the books. Whatever the ethical issue, don't stay in an organization where your ethics and morality are compromised.

You've developed a reputation as a slacker. That reputation is unlikely to change, so you need to carefully consider your options.

You've alienated colleagues. People have to work together well. If you have problems with your coworkers, regardless of your role in that dysfunction, read Daniel Goleman's *Social Intelligence.*[4]

FUSE TIP

Avoid employee relations reruns. It may become your worst late-night TV marathon if you don't move a disrupter out to new places fast. Give them a second chance, but not a third.

What to Do?

If you're having problems at work, do more than just suck it up. As the Reebok ads say, "Life is short. Play hard."

Start with trying to fix what's wrong with your job. Communicating with your boss is always the first step. Have the courage to sit down and have the talk. Don't be paranoid or judgmental. "Just the facts ma'am" is the best approach here. Lay out what you're feeling and, most important, why you're feeling it. Actively listen for feedback.

Don't regard yourself only as a salary slave. If the situation is not reparable, or you can't envision turning what you are doing at work into the career you want, it's time to go. Do what's required as quickly as you can, then network madly to get a jump to a new job.

In the interim, absorb all the training you can and try to develop new skills to take away. There's always something to learn.

Realize that some jobs are not fixable, and it's best to jump ship.

Leaving on Good Terms

Your grandparents probably told you not to burn your bridges. In Boomerspeak, that means not telling people off just for the sake of telling them off. If you're young and on a low rung of the career ladder, you'll likely need a good reference from each job for a few more years. But no matter your age, good references go a long way.

Here are a handful of golden rules for leaving with relationships intact—no matter how tempted you get to slash and burn:

Don't tell off your boss or coworkers, even if they deserve it.

When you leave a job, you might be ticked off—especially if you're leaving on less than optimal terms. You may want to tell people—including your boss—what you truly think of them. Don't do it, even if they deserve it. The six degrees of separation dictate that you'll meet some of them again down the career path and, especially if you stay in the same industry, you may work with them again at a different company.

Don't damage company property, steal, or mess with the IT systems.

Even if you feel used and abused, vandalism, theft, and viruses are criminal offenses. Your professional reputation can be destroyed, and you could end up serving time.

Don't forget to ask for a reference.

This may sound weird if you're leaving your job under bad circumstances. But, since the job will be on your résumé anyway, you should try for a decent reference—in writing.

If you've been fired for malfeasance, don't even ask, but if you're leaving for a less serious reason, ask your boss for a reference despite the job not working out as you both would have liked.

Don't denigrate your organization, boss, or colleagues to whoever replaces you.

Whining will get you nothing. Let your successor figure things out. You may have just had bad chemistry with your former coworkers. Your replacement may have a great experience, even in the same circumstances.

Don't disparage your employer in job interviews.

No one likes a whiner. Your prospective boss will wonder what caused your previous job to go bad, and will suspect it was you.

Get a great new job. The best revenge is living well!

Knowing what to do when your job is not going well can be tricky. All jobs have times when things are iffy to awful. The guideposts above are to help sort out intermittent workplace blues from intolerable workplace ruin. Ride out the former; bail on the latter. If you're a Millennial, ask a Boomer or other mentor for help reading the signs and getting some perspective. Many organizations' HR departments have people to talk with, who must retain confidentiality, and may be able to help you transfer within the organization or report to a different manager. Give yourself a time frame for assessing and acting and stick to it, but make sure that you're seeing the employment picture clearly, not just reacting to unwanted feedback, hurt feelings, or the pitch and yawl of sailing the organizational seas.

CHAPTER 10 **FUSIONS**

- Do more than just suck it up: try to fix what's wrong with your job.
- Communicating with your boss is always the first step. Have the courage to initiate the talk.
- Don't limit your vision to being a salary slave. Always have a Plan B if your job is not working out.
- Leave on the best terms possible. Think six degrees of separation—you likely will work with some of these people again.

CHAPTER 11

Eureka! The Future

By Mary Gavin, President, GavinMedia2.0

"You may as well go big, because it's going to take the same amount of work."
—Mike McCue, CEO, Flipboard

"If we're doing something next year the same way we're doing it this year, then we clearly haven't learned anything."
—Dr. Kevin Stone, entrepreneur and orthopedic surgeon[1]

Time magazine's Person of the Year for 2010 was Millennial Mark Zuckerberg, founder of Facebook. In fewer than seven years, Zuckerberg wired together a twelfth of humanity into a single network that changed the way our species relates to one another.[2] *The Social Network*, the movie about his ascent from student to mogul, was instant Oscar material for its pitch-perfect depiction of Millennials' lives. Its era-defining line is Zuckerberg, giving a legal deposition regarding the complaint that someone else had come up with the idea for an online student directory. To a roomful of top lawyers, he answered dismissively, "My (Facebook) colleagues and I are doing things that no one in this room, including and especially your clients, are intellectually or creatively capable of doing."

'Nuff said.

Many managers and Boomers are genuinely puzzled by Facebook and Millennials' fascination with it. Their corporate policies limit employee use of the site. Limits may be necessary, but the bigger picture of the individual and the network in the workplace—the accelerants of change—has to come into focus.

If you're wondering about your career, your organization, or the business climate going forward, Facebook is a great object lesson. It is wildly popular around the globe because it gives us something we want. A Facebook page is a visa to the World Wide Web: a tool for verifying our identity as we enter a new land. It lets us into the new virtual world and mediates how that world feels to us. It filters the vastness of the Internet to our specific preferences and offers us a 24/7 community network.

Zuckerberg defines the Facebook experience through four words: open . . . connected . . . empathy . . . bandwidth. These words mirror the modern human psyche, especially as modeled by Millennials, both in the workplace and on their own time.

One of the author's sons in northern California

immediately learned of the 2011 earthquake and tsunami in Japan from a high school classmate's Facebook page, where the girl had posted the news from her grandparents in Japan. She quickly added pictures, text, and links to YouTube videos so her network of friends could follow developments through their Facebook pages. She added an information-sharing feed for the high school community and set up ways for everyone to help, including online donations and a fund-raising music concert. On a broader scale, Home Depot launched a Facebook campaign in April 2011 that encourages its "friends" to decide where the company spends its grant dollars and volunteer hours. Every month, the program features four community improvement projects. Home Depot's 250,000+ Facebook fans vote for those projects to determine which one gets a $25,000 Home Depot gift card. All featured projects receive at least $5,000 in gift cards.

Because their marketing firms (staffed by Millennials) have told them to, most major businesses now have a Facebook presence. They can be "liked," interacted with, and added to people's personal networks. Pringles, Coca-Cola, Starbucks, Adidas, Red Bull, Aflac's duck, Oreos, Jones Soda, Burt's Bees, Victoria's Secret, Toyota, Taco Bell, and the NBA are all completely in tune with their audiences on Facebook. They offer up unique content that is frequently refreshed, encourage interaction and engagement, and are fun to use. Check out the Facebook pages of the companies you do business with. Create one for your own organization. Or hire a Millennial to do it.

Ditto for Twitter. It's even sleeker and faster. Twitter is a service that allows users to send out 140-character status updates to a network of followers. It has become an intricate, instant resource for getting info on everything from celebrities' shenanigans to hard news to shopping bargains to corporate rumors to your friends' locations on a Saturday night. Billions of Tweets are being archived by the Library of Congress, sifted for meaning by data-mining companies, and scrutinized by mainstream media for breaking news. Just think of it, immortality and market share, 140 characters at a time. Who is the biggest Tweeter? As of this writing, it's pop sensation Lady Gaga, but everyone from Barack Obama to Ashton Kutcher to General Electric is using the service. Twitter even has a full-time liaison on Capitol Hill, not to lobby but to help the thousands of government employees and politicians already on Twitter to use it better—to create that magical communication that instantly connects constituents to something important to them.

Most organizations are becoming more social through media tools such as Facebook and Twitter. Most industries are going to be rethought so that social design and doing things with friends and colleagues—our network—is at the core of how we work. It will vary widely by industry, but all industries will get to these spaces. If you have any doubt about this, or questions about how to ramp up your own organization, check out our bonus chapter, "It's a Small World After All," by Ayelet Baron, vice president, strategy for Cisco Systems Canada.

You Are Here

As we've said earlier in the book, in our personal lives, all of us as individuals are now at the center of our own universes. Turn on your smartphone and bring up one of the navigation services—Google or Yahoo! Maps. Hit the button that gives you your current location. You are literally at the center of the universe. The world is at your feet. We are all mini Copernicuses, but instead of discovering that the Earth revolves around the Sun, we find that it revolves around our individuality.

Nick Bilton, technology writer for the *New York Times*, published a book at the end of 2010 called *I Live in the Future and Here's How It Works*.[3] He calls this center-of-the-universe phenomenon "me in the middle" and explains the rise of "Me Economics." Being in the center changes everything: your conception of space, time, and location, your sense of place and community, the way you view the news and information on your phone or computer. And it changes your role in transactions. It empowers you to decide quite specifically what to buy, and how to buy and use it rather than simply accepting whatever companies have packaged to sell you. Now you are the starting point. You have the power of being in control.

This has obvious implications in the workplace. Employee experience will need to become increasingly customized, from the on-boarding process to job requirements to benefits. This has not happened yet to any discernible degree. But it will, and it's the Millennials who will make it happen.

The Era of Creative Disruption

Welcome to the second decade of the twenty-first-century, the era of "creative disruption," as John Howkins puts it in *The Creative Economy*. It's a time when individuals are giving free and full rein to their imaginations and reaping the economic value; when people with ideas are more powerful than people with machines; when creative people and organizations are becoming more businesslike, and business is leading the way on creativity.[4]

In the here and now, we have two parallel economies. Companies in the ordinary economy are operating in classic supply-and-demand mode. They have scarce material resources, assert permanent property rights, and compete primarily on price. In the creative economy, individuals and organizations are using resources that are infinite, asserting intellectual rights (which may not be happening in the long term), and are not competing primarily on price. Creativity is their currency.

We have moved from a world of diminishing returns, based on a scarcity of physical objects, to a world of increasing returns based on the infinity of possible ideas and people's genius for using those ideas to generate new products and transactions.[5]

The End of Full Employment and the Rise of Just-in-Time Workers

What does that mean to us as individuals, employers, and members of the four generations still working? In the first quarter of 2011, the global recession showed real signs of lifting. It was led not by manufacturing companies but by web-based companies that transmute people's actions through ideas. Credit became more accessible, due primarily not to banks but to venture capital companies. Enormous IPOs were positioned, led not by technology companies but by companies such as Groupon, the deal-of-the-day website founded in November 2008 and valued at $15 billion two years later.

Out of the rubble of the worst economic times since the Great Depression of the 1930s, a new economy pushed into existence. It had been gestating for the previous ten to fifteen years, unevenly distributed across industries. Its advent was accelerated by the meltdown of financial markets and the demolition of interconnected economies, sort of like the mythical phoenix rising from the ashes.

Buried beneath the twenty-first century's Great Recession, the nature of employment itself has changed. The economic conditions and political considerations favoring large monopolies are fading. The era of full employment is coming to an end. Industrialization spurred the growth of permanent full-time employment; its relative decline is hastening the end of labor-rich workplaces. Full employment is only found statistically now in the public sector, and even the government will start hemorrhaging employees as federal, state, and local governments are unable to fund either current salaries or future retirement obligations. Unemployment numbers will remain stubbornly high despite other signs of economic renewal simply because the way we measure and describe jobs is no longer relevant.

Permanent freelance work, part-time (portfolio) work, and the one-person company (solopreneurs) are all rising as employment vehicles. In creative arenas, they are the dominant employment pattern. In the private sector, the bulk of the creative economy prefers short-term, part-time jobs. Those jobs are being filled by just-in-time workers, who are project-specific consultants with a portfolio of clients and an indefinite time horizon. As work becomes more volatile and specialized, organizations will need to change their mix of workers more frequently.

CNN aired a survey in January 2010 that showed that 80 percent of employees polled were considering changing jobs when the recession ends. Those who still had jobs had dug in but wanted out of the rut once other opportunities came up. If this survey is accurate, the turnover will create a job churn volume unseen since the end of World War II.

It is difficult to manage people in such a changeable

environment. Managing huge numbers of employees out the door without disrupting business is as important as on-boarding newcomers. Managing networks and managing people in isolation are equally important. Managers must handle core full-time employees as well as a raft of just-in-time, project-specific workers. Because nobody is giving them undivided loyalty or depending on them for a steady paycheck, managers will have to work a lot harder to maintain cohesiveness, momentum, and productivity.

FUSE TIP

Full employment is over. The just-in-time workforce is coming, made up of permanent freelancers, part-time workers, and one-person companies (solopreneurs). Be prepared.

Innovation—Video Is the Killer App

From here, change will only accelerate. Facebook is clearly a game changer. Free online video—as on YouTube—will have an even greater impact. There are no language or geographic boundaries to watching someone demonstrate a skill on YouTube, and no costs associated with watching that video repeatedly, in slow-mo if necessary, mastering the skill and then tweaking it and sending it back out to the world.

The curator of the TED talks, Chris Anderson, calls this crowd-accelerated innovation. New global communities now have the means and the motivation to step up their skills and broaden their imaginations. Online video is unleashing an unprecedented wave of innovation in thousands of different disciplines, boosting the net sum of global talent and helping the world get smarter.

Innovation has always been a group activity. But the Internet—and online video free of barriers and costs—has ramped it up to an astonishing degree. When it comes to innovation, size matters. Online video has given every community worldwide reach. People are creating global laboratories for every skill and craft, in a cyclone of improvement. Business writers have various names for it—open innovation, democratizing innovation, collaborative circles, it is reinventing our businesses and our products right now.

And it is being brought into organizations big and small, largely by Millennials.

The Empathic Collaborators

The world has been transformed into a giant global public square. Literally billions of people can connect, collaborate, and create together simultaneously and in real time. Wikipedia describes this as a "global brain"; two billion of these brain cells are young people who have grown up with the Internet as a collaborative medium.[6] Connection, collaboration, and caring are in their DNA. As Jeremy Rifkin describes in *The Empathic Civilization*, their nonhierarchical, networked way of relating; their collaborative nature; their interest in access and inclusion; and their greater sensitivity to diversity predispose Millennials to being the most empathic generation in history.[7]

Young people are bringing their nonhierarchical and collaborative way of thinking into the organizations they work for and are influencing the management styles of some of the world's largest global companies. This has begun big-time at Cisco Systems, for example, which is now a leader in encouraging a more transparent and less top-down approach to management, at General Electric, at Best Buy, and at other organizations we highlight throughout the book.

Other companies are abandoning their pyramids and their twentieth-century command and control structures. (For example, Intel just hired will.i.am of The Black Eyed Peas as its creative director.) In their place, networking and collaborative arrangements are springing up to accommodate the new productivity and market opportunities offered by distributed information and communications technologies, and to welcome a Millennial workforce. That new workforce is proving to be more efficient at collecting information, solving problems, and executing market operations.

An empathic sensibility lies at the heart of the new management style. In the book *The New Leaders*, Daniel Goleman and his coauthors examine the new empathic approach to management that is gaining traction as businesses rethink their conduct in the wake of the colossal failure and near collapse of the global economy.[8]

As Goleman discusses, empathy is the currency of social effectiveness in working life, and the key to the collaborative management style of a twenty-first-century creative economy. It is a critical skill for getting along with diverse workmates and doing business with people from other cultures. As the tasks of leadership become more complex and collaborative, relationship skills become increasingly pivotal.[9] This is collaborative competence in action.

We Ain't Seen Nothin' Yet

In the more than twenty-five years that we've been working in organizational development, we've used Al Jolson's famous words from the first talkie film, *The Jazz Singer*, many times: "You ain't seen nothin' yet." They've never been truer.

In the next five to ten years, the economy will open wide to accelerated innovation, especially in the areas of technology and information technology. Many tens of thousands of Millennials will join the workplace, bringing their individual brands, unique digital skill set, and collaborative outlook. The convergence of ubiquitous broadband, HTML5 (which provides an easy interface to meld text, graphics, and audio/video files), and the consumer demands of immediacy, personalization, networking, and easy access will create a new consumer experience and a new working experience.

This will engender fear and loathing in some, amazement and awe in others. Entire industries will be upended and many careers uprooted.

We don't know what new jobs will be created, but we have described the skills workers will need and the management capabilities organizations must have. The keywords are *cogenerational, connected, creative, collaborative,* and *communities.*

The world of work will never be the same. Or as William Gibson put it, "The future has arrived; it's just not evenly distributed.

CHAPTER 11 **FUSIONS**

- We have moved from a world of diminishing returns, based on a scarcity of physical objects, to a world of increasing returns, based on the infinity of possible ideas.
- The nature of employment has changed. Just-in-time workers are replacing full-time employees. As work becomes more volatile and specialized, organizations will need to change their mix of workers more frequently.
- Literally billions of people can connect, collaborate, and create together simultaneously and in real time

using the Internet. There are no geographic or language barriers and no costs for this crowd-accelerated innovation.

- Ubiquitous broadband, HTML5, and the consumer demands of immediacy, personalization, networking, and easy access will create a new consumer experience and a new working experience.
- The keywords of the future workplace are co-generational, connected, creative, collaborative, and communities.

BONUS CHAPTER

It's a Small World After All

A contribution from Ayelet Baron, VP, Strategy, Cisco Systems Canada

"A Millennial in an Old Vessel,"
—www.Twitter.com/ayeletb

After 26 years in prison with Nelson Mandela, one of the ANC leaders got word that he would be released within the next few weeks. He wasn't sure if it was true or if he would just be transferred to another prison. A few days later the warden called him in and said he had received a fax that stated the prisoner was going to be released the next day. Instead of being elated, the ANC leader asked the warden, "What's a fax? What does that mean?"

Being Connected with the World

Social media is here to stay, but the tools will continue to evolve. We need to understand how the different generations view and use these tools. Some eagerly integrate them into their lives; others resist. Seth Godin says it best in *Small Is the New Big* (Portfolio Hardcover, 2006): "Over and over again, connecting people with one another is what lasts online. Some folks thought it was about technology, but it's not."

The Online and Offline Worlds: What Separates the Generations at Work

With time, the world evolves, and so does technology. Imagine if you were away for just five years and you had to understand all the new shiny objects. Your head would spin. And it's no longer just about the devices; it's also about the applications. Today's services are in the "Cloud." We can share our photos and deepest thoughts online with other people. All this would seem so foreign, and in many cases, it already is.

Millennials are busy with their smartphones. Their notebooks (electronic!) are always open, and they are always plugged into their community, even during meetings. And you often find the Boomers rolling their eyes and being confused about why anyone would prefer to text rather than have a live conversation on the telephone. It even goes deeper. Many Boomers feel that the use of all these devices is contributing to a decline in office etiquette.

Simply said, for Boomers, social media is a place and a set of tools. For Millennials, it is simply a way of everyday life.

Boomers are all about propriety and living offline. They were trained in formalities, taught never to offend. Millennials ignore formalities. Sharing to them means being and living online. The two prevailing rules of this technology generation are (1) actively pursue diversity, and (2) change is good.

A Millennial at Cisco recently said: “My generation is just a bit louder. The older guys are much more formal. They had to worry about ‘big brother,’ and we can’t get information fast enough through our online networks.”

The Facts Today

Business and industry is dominated by: Boomers

Consumer base is dominated by: Xers, Yers

So, What Is Social Media?

People think that social media is new. The hype about it is, but the concept isn’t at all. Early adopters have been connecting with people online since the mid-’80s. A computer considered a dinosaur today made it possible to connect directly with other professionals through The Well and CompuServe in the '90s.

> "I was a systems operator (SYSOP) on CompuServe and ran one online forum and moderated sections in other forums as a 'volunteer.' The connections were mostly based on areas of interest, and people were able to connect professionally, which was why I joined and was active."

Today, with Facebook, it is all about connecting with "friends." LinkedIn is about connecting professionals who you already know and finding the six degrees of separation. Twitter broke away and allows people to connect with other people and strangers; no friendship required. We are about to see new tools coming from both inside and outside of organizations. It will only accelerate as people try to find a more community-based "place" to connect.

Boomers used to get their tools and access to technology at work and then adopt them as consumers. This practice has changed. Today, consumers have access to more tools than what is offered by the organizations that employ them. There is a growing increase by companies to introduce online collaboration tools to provide the same level of online access as people have in their day-to-day lives—Millennials need this more than Boomers do. Millennials want greater transparency and participation in the design of their work because that's what they can do in their lives outside of the workplace.

So, what is "social media" anyway? It's a way

- ✔ For people to be connected online to have conversations and exchange information
- ✔ For consumers to communicate directly and connect with brands and people
- ✔ For brands and organizations to strengthen communities
- ✔ For communications to become viral, via mobile and web based platforms

Social media is *not*

- ✘ A FREE service. It takes time, investment, and engagement.
- ✘ A strategy, on its own, or a solution
- ✘ A way to broadcast information one way
- ✘ A discipline that has "experts" and "gurus"
- ✘ A service driven by tools; people drive the networks

How Do the Generations Engage Online?

- According to Groundswell, 39% of older Boomers are social media "spectators" reading blogs, listening to podcasts, or watching user-generated video.
- Women over 50 are active and vocal about their brands.
- The Pew Research Center's Internet & American Life Project says the median age of Twitter users is 31, which has remained stable over the last year.
- Median age for LinkedIn is now 39.
- Gen X and Boomers also spend time on Flickr and YouTube.
- The largest block of Facebook users are ages 18–25, followed by 26–34 year olds. Together, these groups make up 51% of user population.
- Gen Y is the largest group on Facebook although numbers are rising in the Boomer generation.
- Gen Y is creating more content than any other generation and trusting strangers for where they eat, what movies they watch, and where they travel.

A Set of Tools or a Way to Communicate?

For Boomers, social media is an unknown. It is a "place" that sucks up their time and energy. It's a place where people post updates on what they are eating and doing every minute of their day. Email, for most Boomers, is their comfort zone. The irony is that they did not have access to email all their lives, but they are reluctant to give it up today and try other tools that are far more effective. They avoid collaborating because they have spent most of their lives being trained to control information. They created the notion of cascading information to the employee base. Is it any wonder that Boomers in management spend so much time in meetings to discuss how to achieve greater collaboration?

For Millennials, social media is part of their day-to-day life. They were born at a time when connectivity was a given. And wherever they are in the world, as long as they have some device with which to connect to the Internet, they can be online. They've always had it. They see the tools as a place where they live and connect with people. Technology is simply a part of their DNA. It's integrated in their daily life, not something they need to think about using. The device they connect with needs to have the latest applications and the fastest way to connect with others.

The disconnect in the workplace is not about whether or not to use social media at work for the Millennials; rather it is about having the same access in their professional lives that they have in their personal lives. It's simply how they work and live. They work with large networks and use multiple modes of communication during the day. They also do not like hierarchy and view everyone in their organization as colleagues to collaborate with online and offline.

Boomers write long blog posts on how Millennials don't "get" what real work is about and have a sense of entitlement because they feel threatened. Millennials have a way of driving Boomers crazy. Recently, two prestigious publications featured articles intended to demonstrate what's wrong with the younger generation: "What Is It About Twenty-Somethings? Why Are So Many People in Their Twenties Taking So Long to Grow Up?" (*New York Times*, August 18, 2010) and "Two Common Mistakes of Millennials at Work" (*Harvard Business Review*, August 30, 2010).

What they don't explore is that it is just a different view of the world. For Millennials, email is insignificant. They expect immediate response to their emails because that's how they live. They know their management is busy and, too often, feel bad when they take away the time they should be focused on making money and doing their job. One Millennial recently observed that he has seen management have back-to-back meetings five days a week; there is never a break. And although he sees them on Instant Messaging, he doesn't feel comfortable interrupting. What does this mean? It means that the formality is a real barrier to communication across generations. This Millennial is wishing his management knew how to talk to people in real time.

"When I lead webinars on social media, one of the questions that always comes up is 'How do you keep your personal and professional lives separate in the age of social media?' I always know that this question is being asked by a Boomer. For Boomers, mixing the two is a negative. They were brought up with that instinctive need to separate."

So What's Happening?

It is exciting to have Millennials in the workforce because they communicate in real time. They want to be part of communities and be able to go back to content whenever they need, not archive and search for emails. Over time, they will bring everyone to collaboration spaces, and email and mailing lists will wither. They are our future business leaders and will demonstrate leadership when it comes to online collaboration. Will they always be right? No. Do they know which tools will become predominant? No. But that's not the point.

A Millennial recently shared that she feels constrained at work because her management said she is not allowed to talk to anyone in the organization more senior than her direct manager. Odds are she will leave the company in a few years, especially when the economy gets stronger. On the other hand, a Boomer shared that his daughter, after spending four weeks as an intern at his office, said his generation works too hard and she is happy that she will never put work first. She also said she felt that his office environment was constraining because of the policy that does not allow employees to connect to social media sites from work.

A colleague who has been recruiting candidates online recently shared her thoughts on the generations at work on her Facebook account. Sedef M. Buyukataman, one of the best recruiters at Cisco Systems, posted this on her wall as a result of an IM conversation where she was asked: "What are the key disconnects that you see today when it comes to the different generations at work?"

> Millennials get a lot of flack for being difficult and demanding because they're less tied to the traditions of the past. They work more efficiently, challenge authority and understand teamwork better than any generation before. They thrive off of feedback! Sad that many managers are afraid of them. We should be embracing their work style and communication networks as a benchmark of excellence.
>
> What I like most about this generation is that everyone has an equal voice at the table, they are not concerned with titles or status—it's about the content of what you have to add to the conversation. They cannot survive without communication and feedback and social networks are proof of this. People who can't take the heat and learn from others have

> no place in the workplace of tomorrow and this will improve everyone's life and create a more accountable and ethical world. Well done!

Millennials are the first generation to have access to the same tools that business uses to get work done, and a lot more that organizations have yet to adopt. For them, information flows in all directions.

What Change Will Mean

We have many generations in the workplace today. There is a growing divide between them, but it comes from how they have been socialized and what access they've had to technology as part of their daily lives.

The discipline of change management was created as technology started to enter the workplace. Departments and consulting practices sprouted across the world to help employees adapt to new systems and processes, like implementations of SAP, Oracle, and www.Salesforce.com. The question became how can we move employees from being aware of the change that needs to take place to the internalization of the change in how they work every day and adopting the new tools and processes?

Today, at a job interview, Millennials want to know what device is offered as part of their employment package. They want to understand the level of connectivity, ability to work remotely, policies around social media, mobility, and how much time off they will get. Their needs and interests are simply different from those of Boomers. They want to connect with others online and collaborate. They hate email and voice mail. They want to be able to SMS and text. And, it's no longer an issue whether this is right or wrong. It just is.

New technology creates more networked and less hierarchical workplaces. Work is distributed across more people in more locations. Boomers have experienced the movement of how teams work virtually, across time zones and cultures. Millennials live in a connected world and working virtually comes naturally to most of them. That does not mean they don't enjoy and need face-to-face interaction; they need both. They have interchangeable work styles. They can get their work done where and when they need or want to.

The Boomers say, "I don't have time for Instant Messaging since I am in back-to-back meetings all day." They see it as an extra activity, not integrated into their daily routine. The Millennials need a translator when they hear this and ask: "What does that mean? Why would you need time to IM?" This disconnect is because this is a way of life to them right now.

Our World Is Changing: New Realities to Contend With

A number of trends are making business more complex, creating a need for individuals and their organizations to change the way they work.

Globalization has enabled organizations to tap into worldwide talent pools and reach new markets, but at the same time, it has dispersed working teams across the globe and forced a less personal, more asynchronous way of working for those not using online tools that can connect them anytime, anywhere. For Boomers, it's harder to connect with the people they need when they need them. It's harder to resolve issues over distance and build trust with team members who you don't know well and/or can't see in person. The "out of sight, out of mind" issue can become a real problem, as it's difficult for team members to understand what their counterparts are working on at any given time. For Millennials, again, being connected and in constant communication helps feed their curiosity and constant need to feel connected.

If the '90s spawned "The Information Age," today we're living in "The Participation Age"—Web 2.0 tools like video portals, podcasts, blogs, wikis, and discussion forums are changing the face of how information is created, published, managed, and consumed. While this has led to tremendous productivity gains, organizations are now challenged with managing information overload, accuracy, and relevance to ensure that their employees are connecting with the right content and expertise when they need it.

Today's workforce is accustomed to new ways of interacting and sharing knowledge, but they're being confined to work with a tool set that stifles their productivity. As a result, many employees are using consumer-based applications like Facebook for business interactions, which also pose challenges around enterprise security and compliance.

It can feel to Millennials like they are working in the dark sometimes. The irony is they genuinely want to learn from the older and savvier team members.

Cisco Quad: Experience a New Way to Work

I have been very fortunate to work at a company that is on the bleeding edge of technology. It allows me to experience and introduce solutions that our customers will be adopting. When people ask me, what will you be doing in the next five years? I tell them, "Allowing Cisco customers to experience the future."

Cisco Quad helps solve the challenges of mobility, social networking, and dispersed teams. This enterprise collaboration platform combines the power of social networking with communications, business information, and content management systems. At the same time, it meets IT's needs for policy management, scalability, security, and ease of management.

Quad helps my team:

- **Improve productivity** by optimizing all aspects of the employee lifecycle. Quickly and efficiently attract, hire, and train new employees; scale expertise and encourage engagement; and transfer knowledge once employees leave.
- **Enhance innovation** by improving product development. Build environments to encourage employee participation, get new and better ideas, protect sensitive documents and materials, and move products to market faster.
- **Generate growth** by accelerating sales cycles. Customize communities and content around specific sales opportunities, make specialists and other subject matter experts more available and accessible to people in the field, share best practices, and lessons learned, and drive a collaborative sales culture.
- And the best part is that it will be available on my Smartphone and iPad real soon. It supports mobility.

How to Recruit and Retain Millennials with Social Media

To be able to attract and retain Millennial employees, it is helpful to understand some of what they view as important. For example:

- ➔ They want to be able to respect their manager.
- ➔ They want to enjoy working with the people around them.
- ➔ They want to have access to innovative tools and technologies.
- ➔ They want a work-life balance.
- ➔ They want to know about career paths and career advancement.
- ➔ They want to know how much vacation time they get.

Boomers may think these desires are ridiculous, but it is what is important to Millennials. It means that we need to introduce some programs that are appealing to them and always include online collaboration.

At Cisco, I introduced a Reverse Mentoring program where the Generation Y mentored our senior executives. The goal of the program was to share knowledge on social media, new ways of collaborating and ways of doing business, and their impact on business. It was a great experience, and what I found was that this generation is fearless. They were able to mentor very senior executives and be very upfront and honest with their feedback. What they accomplished was preparing our leaders for the next generation of employees and increasing executive diversity awareness by providing leaders with an opportunity to increase their understanding, communication, comfort level, and appreciation of the different ways in working with Millennials.

They didn't do this alone. We spent a lot of time together. Millennials also require mentorship and guidance. You need to understand what drives and motivates them at work.

Make sure you go where they are. They Google everything. Also go to sites like http://www.glassdoor.com to find out what employees say about your company. You should know where they are and educate yourself on the tools. If you leave Millennial employees voice mail messages you will not hear from them. They tune out any communication effort they perceive as unsolicited or spam. And, if by any chance they do respond, they will do so via email.

What's Ahead?

Work will never be the same. Thank goodness. Sharing is the new normal. It will take time, but as the economy recovers, more employees retire, and a new force enters the mix, change will be prevalent. The key is to get ready for the changes by focusing on the business and redefining the employment contract based on needs and drivers. Online collaboration and social media are actually good things.

The '90s had a revolving door of focus on how knowledge should be captured. How knowledge will be tracked. No one has figured it out . . . yet. Where have all the chief knowledge officers gone? I hope that we will not see a new flood of chief collaboration officers. Why?

Because collaboration should not be delegated. It needs to be integrated into the business. Why would you have someone in charge of tools?

Millennials are the leaders of the future, but today's leaders still need to guide them in the ways of the workplace. They also need to encourage all generations to become involved in common enterprise-wide platforms that can develop and enrich working relationships and networks.

As mentioned earlier, there is a lot of hype about social media right now, which has created some confusion around when to strategically use it. The key is to realize that for any organization, social media is another channel to drive trusted relationships and community interactions. It's important for any organization to have a plan that maps out their overall journey through a vision, a strategy, and an executable road map.

> "A revolution doesn't happen when society adopts new tools, it happens when society adopts new behaviors." —Clay Shirky

Onward!

"Don't trust anyone over thirty."
—1964, Jack Weinberg, student at UC Berkeley (born 1940)

"Don't trust anyone over twenty."
—2008, Stephen Hannan, student at Saint Mark's School (born 1995)

As Alan Kay said, "The best way to predict the future is to create it." The watchwords of the future that we see are cogenerational, connected, creative, collaborative, and communities. These concepts will continue to transform the nature of work across every industry. As John Howkins details in *The Creative Economy*, the keys to competitive success are now human and virtual intelligence; creativity; the ability to accurately assess the motivational profiles of clients, customers, colleagues, and vendors; global outlook in terms of influences, markets, and resources; just-in-time innovation; and truly collaborative relationships.[1]

To unlock that future, organizations need to unleash and leverage the capabilities of each worker, playing off the experience and unique strengths of those in both generations.

In other words, when Boomers' experience, perseverance, and social conscience fuse with Millennials' boundary-less perspective, technological wizardry, and need for meaningful work, a better future for the organization is created.

It is a revolutionary time. The first workplace revolution traded farms for factories. The second swapped muscles for minds. The third revolution, happening now, is the shift from left-brain to right-brain creative economic production, a shift brought on by the World Wide Web and its digitization, connectivity, and globalization. Ayelet Baron of Cisco Systems Canada calls this the "Participation Age" in her bonus chapter on social media.

We believe that Boomers will be the midwives and enablers of this shift; Millennials will be the producers. Their unique core competencies are a perfect fit to prime the global creative economy.

The United States is at the forefront of this new world. Our creative sector now accounts for more than $2 trillion—nearly half of all wages and salaries paid in the United States. Over the next decade, this country expects to add 10 million more creative-sector jobs. At the current rate of increase, the number of creative jobs will soon eclipse the number of manufacturing jobs.[2]

This has changed the rules of competition.

The true source of value creation is creative talent, especially that of the Millennials. As we said earlier, this generation has been shaped not by understanding the natural world and manipulating its resources but by artificial intelligence and virtual relationships. *Organizations that recruit and motivate their own creative workers will win.*

Resources matter. There's a reason why Google attracts the best and the brightest. The hard and soft cutting-edge technology it offers employees, plus excellent salaries and benefits and world-class colleagues, has created a culture that optimizes each employee's potential and contribution and offers an incubator for each worker's ideas and innovations.

But accessing the creative economy is not limited to the most educated and creative workers, or to emerging technology companies. The creative economy is endemic in today's world.

Many retail organizations operating across the globe—Starbucks, Whole Foods, Target, Best Buy—are trying to enable employees to jump service work into the space of innovation and creativity. Richard Florida writes, "Small changes made on the salesroom floor—by a Millennial sales rep reconceiving a Vonage display or an immigrant salesperson acting to increase outreach, advertising, and service to non-English-speaking communities—have been implemented nationwide, generating hundreds of millions of dollars in added revenue."[3] These forward-thinking companies are ramping up pay and creating workplaces where employees can use their unique perspectives and creative talents to enrich customer experiences and generate additional revenues. Best Buy's value statements say it all: The company's goal is "[to] provide opportunities for employees to bring forward new ideas, new thinking . . . [for] each employee to contribute their unique ideas and experiences in service of customers . . . [to] unleash the power of our people . . . [and to] have fun while being the best."[4]

What will our organizations look like when they can do all this?[5]

They will reflect imagination and innovation in products and services, in production and marketing, in workplaces and practices. They will show commitment to human capital, community, and environmental sustainability.

And what of each of us, Millennial or Boomer or somewhere in between? We also have choices to make as individuals in doing the work that defines us, creating organizations that sustain us, contributing our best work, finding meaning in that work, and making a difference in social and community causes.

The choices we make for our organizations and ourselves will inform and create the future.

"It seems to go right down to the heart of human nature—what we workers get out of our jobs intrinsically, emotionally, and physically."
—Matt Finkelstein, FutureSense blog post

NOTES

Forward!

1 Tamara Erickson, *Retire Retirement: Career Strategies for the Boomer Generation* (Boston: Harvard Business Press, 2008).

2 Daniel Pink, *A Whole New Mind: Moving from the Information Age to the Conceptual Age* (New York City: Riverhead Trade, 2006).

3 See Neil Howe & William Strauss, *Generations: The History of America's Future, 1584-2069* (New York: William Morrow 1991) and Neil Howe & William Strauss, *Millennials Rising: The Next Generation* (New York: Vintage Books 2000); John C. Beck & Mitchell Wade, *Got Game: How the Gamer Generation Is Reshaping Business Forever* (Boston: Harvard Business Press 2004); Ben Rigby, *Mobilizing Generation 2.0: A Practical Guide to Using Web 2.0: Technologies to Recruit, Organize, and Engage Youth* (San Francisco: John Wiley & Sons 2008), Jean Twenge, *Generation Me: Why Today's Young Americans Are More Confident, Assertive, Entitled—and More Miserable Than Ever Before* (New York: Free Press 2006);
<http://www.marcprensky.com>; <http://www.mccrindle.com.au>;
<http://www.brazencareerist.com>

Chapter 1

1 There are many different ways to define Millennials, and those variations are often disputed. The way that makes the most sense to us is to include the 80 million Americans roughly between the ages of 15 and 30, born largely between 1980 and 1995.

2 Marc Pensky, "The Wisdom (and Worth) of 'Generation Techs,'" *Strategy & Business*, 08/25/04
< http://www.strategy-business.com/article/04314?gko=7489b

3 John Naisbitt, *Megatrends: Ten New Directions Transforming Our Lives* (New York City: Grand Central Publishing, 1988).

4 Rob Johnson, "The Entitlement Generation," 12/05; <http://www.fsu.com/pages/2005/09/29/workplace_tensions.html>; "Statistics on the Quarterlife Crisis, Twentysomethings, and Young Adults," *Quarterlife Crisis.*

5 John C. Beck and Mitchell Wade, *Got Game: How the Gamer Generation is Reshaping Business Forever* (Boston: Harvard Business Press, 2004); Jean M. Twenge, *Generation Me: Why Today's Young Americans Are More Confident, Assertive, Entitled—and More Miserable Than Ever Before* (New York City: Free Press, 2007).

6 Beck and Wade, 1-26.

7 Nadira Hira, "Attracting the Twentysomething Worker," *Fortune*, 05/15/07.

8 Russ Eckel, "Learning Along with the Millennials," 2008 <http://downloads.generationsatwork°/training.pdf >

9 Cam Marston, "Myths About Millennials," www.About.com <http://humanresources.about.com/od/managementtips/a/millennial_myth_2.htm>

10 Jim Finkelstein and Mary Gavin, *Fuse: Igniting the Full Power of the Creative Economy*, 2009.

11 Sally Kane, "Baby Boomers," www.About.com <http://legalcareers.about.com/od/practicetips/a/Babyboomers.htm>

Chapter 2

1 Robert Allen, "Managers Must Set Example for Gen Y Kidployees," *Nation's Restaurant News.* 10/10/05 <http://findarticles.com/p/articles/mi_m3190/is_41_39/ai_n15722192/>

2 Mark McCrindle, "The New Generations at Work: Attracting, Recruiting, Retaining & Training Generation Y," McCrindle Research

3 Benson, Levinson, and Allison, "Millennials, Brands, and Businesses," *Brand Blueprint.* 2006 <http://www.brandblueprint.com/articles/Millennials_Brands_and_Business.pdf >

4 Ryan Healy, "3 More New Marketing Rules for Recruiting Millennials," *Employee Evolution.* 2/14/08 <http://www.employeeevolution.com/archives/2008/02/14/3-more-new-marketing-rules-for-recruiting-millennials/>

5 http://www.retailcustomerexperience.com/article_print/4159/Hiring-Millennials-requires-openness-immediacy

6 Carolyn A. Martin and Bruce Tulgan, *Managing the Generation Mix: From Collision to Collaboration* (Amherst: HRD Press, 2002); Mark McCrindle, "The New Generations at Work: Attracting, Recruiting, Retaining & Training Generation Y," McCrindle Research <http://www.mccrindle.com.au/RESOURCES/WP_NewGenAtWork.pdf>; <http://www.pizzamarketplace.com/article/102675/NRA-Show-Hiring-Millennials-requires-openness-immediacy>

7 Penelope Trunk, "Why You Should Never Complain About Your Company," 05/13/2008 <http://blog.penelopetrunk.com/2008/05/13/why-you-should-never-complain-about-your-company/>

8 Shriram Harid, "Despite Lack of Work, Millennial Generation Remains Bouyant," 02/26/10 <http://www.huffingtonpost.com/2010/02/26/despite lack of work mill_n_478865.html>

9 Marc Prensky, “Digital Natives Digital Immigrants” 2001 <http://www.marcprensky.com/writing/Prensky%20-%20Digital%20Natives,%20Digital%20Immigrants%20-%20Part1.pdf>

10 “Column 8,” The Sydney Morning Herald, <http://www.smh.com.au/opinion/column8>

11 Andrew McAfee, “How Millennials’ Sharing Habits Can Benefit Organizations” 08/23/10 <http://blogs.hbr.org/hbr/mcafee/2010/08/how-millennials-sharing-habits.html>

12 “Generation Y: The Millennials Ready or Not, Here They Come,” NAS Insights, 2006 <http://www.scribd.com/doc/2607132/GENERATION-Y-THE-MILLENNIALS>

13 Jim Finkelstein, quoted in “The Ultimate Mashup: An Interview with Jim Finkelstein, Author of *Fuse*,” *Wisepreneur* <http://wisepreneur.com/leading-innovation/the-ultimate-mashup-an-interview-with-jimfinkelstein-author-of-fuse>

14 Shriram Harid, “Millennial Generation Remains Buoyant”

15 David Hakala, “10 Must-Read Online-Recruiting Blogs” 04/03/08 <http://www.hrworld.com/features/10-online-recruiting-blogs-040308>

Chapter 3

1 Kathyrn Tyler, “The Tethered Generation,” *HR Magazine*, 05/01/07; Nadira Hira, “Attracting the Twentysomething Worker,” *Fortune*, 5/28/07.

2 Nadira Hira, “Attracting the Twentysomething Worker,” *Fortune*, 5/28/07.

3 Jim Heskett, “How Will Millennials Manage?” 08/02/07 <http://hbswk.hbs.edu/item/5736.html>

4 Peter Sheahan, quoted in “What Millennial Workers Want: How to Attract and Retain Gen Y Employees,” Robert Half International, YAHOO! Hotjobs <http://www.hotjobsresources.com/pdfs/MillennialWorkers.pdf>

5 Robert W. Wendover, “Getting Millennials to Engage,” CPCU Society <http://www.cpcusociety.org/page/135618/index.v3page;jsessionid=36e2f7e7ec5>

6 Copthorne MacDonald, review of Michael Lerner’s *Spirit Matters: Global Healing and the Wisdom of the Soul* (Charlottesville: Hampton Roads Publishing Co., 2000), *Integralis: Journal of Integral.*

7 Beyond.com <http://www.beyond.com/Media/Generation-Y-In-The-Workplace.asp>; Brazen Careerist, 05/23/08 <http://www.BrazenCareerist.com>

8 Marc Prensky, “Capturing the Value of ‘Generation Tech’ Employees,” 06/30/04 <http://www.strategy-business.com/media/file/enews-06-30-04.pdf>

9 Marc Prensky, “Digital Natives Digital Immigrants,” 2001.

10 Marc Presky, “The Emerging Online Life Of The Digital Native,” 2004 <http://www.marcprensky.com/writing/Prensky-The_Emerging_Online_Life_of_the_Digital_Native-03.pdf>

11 Lee Cockerell, "They Have Some Big Plans," 12/16/10 <http://blog.leecockerell.com/?p=975>

12 Mark McCrindle, "Seriously Cool: Marketing and Communicating with Diverse Generations" <http://www.mccrindle.com.au/RESOURCES/WP_Seriously-Cool_MarketingCommunicating-with-Diverse-Generations.pdf>

Chapter 4

1 Penelope Trunk, "Don't Wait for Retirement to Live the Good Life. Do it Now," 03/20/08 <http://blog.penelopetrunk.com/2008/03/20/dont-wait-for-retirement-to-live-the-good-life-do-it-now/>

2 Michelle Conlin, "Youthquake," *Bloomberg Businessweek*, 01/09/08 <http://www.businessweek.com/magazine/content/08_03/b4067000290367.htm>; <http://mobilize.org/?tray=content&tid=top364&cid=11DS10>

3 Ibid.

4 Bureau of Labor Statistics, "Economic News Release: Table A-1: Current and real (constant 1982-1984 dollars) earnings for all employees on private nonfarm payrolls, seasonally adjusted," 5/13/2011 < http://www.bls.gov/>

5 Shari Caudron, "Master the Compensation Maze," *Workforce Management*, 1993 <http://www.workforce.com/archive/feature/22/18/22/index.php>

Chapter 5

1 Michelle Conlin, "Youthquake."

2 Art Brooks, "Compensation and Benefits for Generations X and Y," 02/08 <http://www.talentmgt.com/compensation_benefits/2008/February/542/index.php?pt=a&aid=542&start=3088&page=2>

3 Rebecca R. Hastings, "The Ideal Workplace for Generation Y," SHRM, 12/01/06 <http://www.shrm.org/hrdisciplines/Diversity/Articles/Pages/CMS_019637.aspx>

4 "What Millennial Workers Want: How to Attract and Retain Gen Y Employees," Robert Half International, YAHOO! Hotjobs <http://www.hotjobsresources.com/pdfs/MillennialWorkers.pdf>

Chapter 6

1 Heather Knight, "98-Year-Old Graduate Has Whirlwind Day," SFGate.com 06/15/2006.

2 Courtney Reimer, "Cutting the Bull Out of Corporate Jargon," *Columbia News*, 01/07/06 <http://www.azcentral.com/ent/pop/articles/0107jargon0107-CR.html>

3 "Fake + Blog = FLOG," *The Pursuit of Techyness*, 07/15/08 <http://techyness.com/tag/flog/

4 Philip Hertzler, "Communicating with the Millennials: Hunh? What Makes You Think They Are Reading Your Stuff?" 09/01/07 <http://www.jackconsultingllc.com>

5 Philip Hertzler, "Communicating with the Millennials."

6 Andrew Tilin, "How to Speak Millennial: Lessons From a B-School Dean," 05/16/08 <http://www.bnet.com/2403-13059_23-201746.html>

7 "Boomers Embracing Technology Faster Than Ever," *The Savvy Boomer,* 03/28/2009 <http://www.thesavvyboomer.com/the_savvy_boomer/2009/03/boomers-embracing-technology-fasterthan-ever.html>

8 Nina Kim, "12 Things to Never Say to Younger and Older Coworkers," *Excelle* <http://excelle.monster.com/benefits/articles/4245-12-things-to-never-say-to-younger-and-oldercoworkers?page=8>

9 Nina Kim, "12 Things to Never Say to Younger and Older Coworkers," *Excelle* <http://excelle.monster.com/benefits/articles/4245-12-things-to-never-say-to-younger-and-older-coworkers?page=8>

10 Michelle V. Rafter, "Jhobby, Playcheck, and Other Boomer Lingo," *SecondAct,* 06/22/10 <http://www.secondact.com/2010/06/jhobby-playcheck-and-other-lingo-from-the-new-retirement-boom/>

Chapter 7

1 "The Google Culture," Google.com <http://www.google.com/corporate/culture.html>

Chapter 8

1 Dennis Cauchon, "Gender Pay Gap is Smallest on Record," *USA Today,* 09/14/10 <http://www.usatoday.com/money/workplace/2010-09-13-wage-gaps_N.htm>

2 Alan Kopit, "Research Reveals Rise in Interoffice Romance," Lawyers.com <http://research.lawyers.com/Research-Reveals-Rise-in-Interoffice-Romance.html>

3 "Nine Biggest Myths of the Workplace by Penelope Trunk," 05/18/07 <http://blog.guykawasaki.com/2007/05/the_nine_bigges.html>

4 Max Messmer, "Myth Busters: Breaking through Workplace Misconceptions," *Strategic Finance,* 07/01/06 <http://www.allbusiness.com/finance/3592324-1.>

5 Brian Amble, "Boomer or Slacker, We're All the Same," *Management-Issues,* 05/08/07 <http://www.management-issues.com/2007/5/8/research/boomer-or-slacker-were-all-the-same.asp>

Chapter 9

1 "Casual vs. Professional Attire in the Workplace–What Message Are YOU Sending?" *AppleOne* <http://www.appleone.com/Career_Seekers/ToolsAndResources/Core/core_17.aspx>

2 "Coverage Under the FLSA," <http://www.flsa.com/coverage.html>

3 Dan Malachowski, "Wasted Time at Work Costing Companies Billions," Salary.com 07/11/05 <http://www.sfgate.com/cgi-bin/article.cgi?f=g/a/2005/07/11/wastingtime.TMP>

4 U.S. Department of Labor, "Work Hours," <http://www.dol.gov>

5 Donald K. Burleson, "Personal Dress Code Tips," Burleson Consulting <http://www.dba-oracle.com/dress_code.htm>

6 Clint Greenleaf, *The Unwritten Rules of the Workplace* (Austin: Emerald Book Company, 2010).

7 "Employment Background Checks: A Jobseeker's Guide," *Privacy Rights Clearinghouse* 10/10 <http://www.privacyrights.org/fs/fs16-bck.htm#2>

Chapter 10

1 Anne Altman, "Tips from a Bitter Temp," *Bloomberg Businessweek,* 08/14/08 <http://www.businessweek.com/magazine/content/08_34/b4097059792102.htm>

2 Dawn Rosenberg McKay, "Is It Time to Quit Your Job?" About.com <http://careerplanning.about.com/od/quittingyourjob/a/when_to_quit.htm>; Susan M. Heathfield, "Top Ten Reasons to Quit Your Job," About.com <http://humanresources.about.com/od/whenemploymentends/a/quit_job_3.htm>

3 Robert I. Sutton, *The No A**hole Rule: Building a Civilized Workplace and Surviving One That Isn't* (New York City: Business Plus, 2007).

4 Daniel Goleman, *Social Intelligence: The New Science of Human Relationships* (New York City: Bantam, 2006).

Chapter 11

1 Sam Whiting, "Inventor Never Stops Operating," *SFGate.com,* 01/16/11 <http://articles.sfgate.com/2011-01-16/news/27032083_1_orthopedic-surgeon-invention-stone-clinic>

2 Lev Grossman, "Person of the Year 2010: Mark Zuckerberg," *Time Magazine,* 12/15/10 <http://www.time.com/time/specials/packages/article/0,28804,2036683_2037183,00.html>

3 Nick Bilton, *I Live in the Future and Here's How It Works: Why Your World, Work, and Brain Are Being Creatively Disrupted* (New York City: Crown Business, 2010).

4 John Howkins, *The Creative Economy* (Penguin Global: 2007) 9, 12

5 Ibid., 129-130.

6 Dan Tapscott and Anthony D. Williams, *Wikinomics: How Mass Collaboration Changes Everything* (New York: Penguin, 2008) 41, 47.

7 Jeremy Rifkin, *The Empathic Civilization: The Race to Global Consciousness in a World in Crisis* (New York: Tarcher, 2009) 543.

8 Daniel Goleman, Richard E. Boyatzis, and Annie McKee, *The New Leaders* (New York City: Little Brown, 2003)

9 Ibid.

Onward

1 We are informed here by many works that envision innovation and future thinking, including C.K. Prahalad and M.S. Krishnan, *The New Age of Innovation: Driving Co-created Value through Global Networks* (New York: McGraw Hill 2008); Clayton Christensen, *The Innovator's Dilemma: When New Technologies Cause Great Firms to Fail* (Boston: Harvard Business School Press 1997); Clayton Christensen and Michael Raynor, *The Innovator's Solution: Creating and Sustaining Successful Growth* (Boston: Harvard Business School Press 2003)

2 Richard Florida, "A Search for Jobs in Some of the Wrong Places," *USA Today*, 02/12/06 <http://www.usatoday.com/news/opinion/editorials/2006-02-12-bush-jobs_x.htm>

3 Richard Florida, "The Future of the American Workforce in the Global Creative Economy," *Cato Unbound*, 06/04/06 <http://www.cato-unbound.org/2006/06/04/richard-florida/the-future-of-the-american-workforce-in-the-global-creative-economy>

4 "Corporate Responsibility: Our Aspirations and Fiscal 2008 Performance Report," Best Buy <http://www.bby.com/cmn/files/CSR_2008_Final.pdf>

5 Robert J. Laubacher, Thomas W. Malone, and the MIT Scenario Working Group, "Two Scenarios for 21st Century Organizations: Shifting Networks of Small Firms or All-Encompassing 'Virtual Countries'" 01/97 <http://ccs.mit.edu/21c/21cwpmain.html>

INDEX

D

E

F

G

H

Q

R

S

T

U

V

W

Y

Z

ABOUT THE AUTHORS

Boomer Jim Finkelstein's experience has included being a partner in a Big Five firm, a CEO of a professional services firm, a corporate executive for Fortune 500 companies, and an entrepreneur as president and CEO of FutureSense, Inc. During his thirty-four-plus years of consulting and corporate experience, he has specialized in business and people strategy, motivation and reward, and organizational assessment, development, communications, and transformation. He has worked for diverse industries—from health care to high tech—and has built programs and provided services to boards of directors, senior executives, management, and frontline employees.

Jim earned a BA in psychology and economics from Trinity College in Hartford, Connecticut, and his MBA in organization behavior and development from the Wharton School of the University of Pennsylvania.

He notes, "Throughout my career, I have been called everything from a visionary to a contrarian. I continue to believe that businesses and organizations need to think 'off the edge of the paper' in order to assure themselves of the most favorable solutions and outcomes. I also believe that determining the unique *right* practices for each situation is preferred to 'flocking like sheep to the slaughter' by following perceived *best* practices. In fact, they are, at best, 'interesting practices.' What works for one organization may not work for another!"

Jim has enjoyed being a soccer and basketball coach and team manager for more than fifteen years and is still a very active soccer referee for adult, high school, and youth matches. Since his youth, he's been inspired by these words of Edward Everett Hale: "I am only one, but still I am one. I cannot do everything, but still I can do something; and because I cannot do everything, I will not refuse to do the something I can do."

You can contact Jim at jim@futuresense.com.

Mary Gavin is President of Gavin Media 2.0, a firm specializing in communications that integrate the arts of strategy, content, design, and new media. With more than twenty-five years of experience in goal-oriented, executive-level communications, she is most interested these days in fusing high tech–media 2.0 webspaces and interactive designs—with high touch—elegant, lucid content for communications, board materials, client campaigns, and books.

Mary's résumé spans law, financial services, alternative energy, e-commerce, regulated industries, and consulting.

She has designed and implemented successful communications strategies for Fortune 500 companies, national nonprofits, and government organizations. Serving both in-house and as a consultant, Mary has been head of Executive Communications for Bank of America; and Director of Communications for the Bar Association of San Francisco, SunPower/SPG Solar, and FutureSense, Inc.

In addition to her business experience, she holds a JD from the School of Law at the University of California, Davis, where she was Executive Editor of the Law Review, and a BA from the George Washington University in Washington, DC. Mary is the editor or contributor to books on economics, contract law, jurisprudence, media, mergers and acquisitions post-closing practices, and the Report to the White House on "The Status of Pro Bono and Diversity in the Legal Profession," as well as coauthor of *Fuse* with Jim.

You can contact Mary through her webspace, www.gavinmedia.org.

About FutureSense

FutureSense, Inc., is a management advisory and consulting firm specializing in the areas of organization and people. They advise clients on how to build and sustain their human capital capacity and improve organizational performance by attracting, developing, engaging, motivating, and retaining employees. You can learn more about FutureSense at www.futuresense.com.